EYE ON
Art

WALT DISNEY

by Barbara Sheen

LUCENT BOOKS
A part of Gale, Cengage Learning

GALE
CENGAGE Learning

Detroit • New York • San Francisco • New Haven, Conn • Waterville, Maine • London

© 2014 Gale, Cengage Learning

WCN: 01-100-101

LIBRARY OF CONGRESS CATALOGING-IN-PUBLICATION DATA

Sheen, Barbara, author.
  Walt Disney / by Barbara Sheen.
    pages cm. -- (Eye on art)
  Summary: "These books provide a historical overview of the development of different types of art and artistic movements; explore the roots and influences of the genre; discuss the pioneers of the art and consider the changes the genre has undergone"-- Provided by publisher.
  Includes bibliographical references and index.
  ISBN 978-1-4205-0898-7 (hardback)
  1. Disney, Walt, 1901-1966--Juvenile literature. 2. Animators--United States--Biography--Juvenile literature. 3. Animated films--United States--Juvenile literature. I. Title.
  NC1766.U52D559 2013
  791.43092--dc23
  [B]
                                                        2013038452

Lucent Books
27500 Drake Rd
Farmington Hills MI 48331

ISBN-13: 978-1-4205-0898-7
ISBN-10: 1-4205-0898-9

Printed in the United States of America
1 2 3 4 5 6 7 17 16 15 14 13

CONTENTS

Foreword

Some thirty-one thousand years ago, early humans painted strikingly sophisticated images of horses, bison, rhinoceroses, bears, and other animals on the walls of a cave in southern France. The meaning of these elaborate pictures is unknown, although some experts speculate that they held ceremonial significance. Regardless of their intended purpose, the Chauvet-Pont-d'Arc cave paintings represent some of the first known expressions of the artistic impulse.

From the Paleolithic era to the present day, human beings have continued to create works of visual art. Artists have developed painting, drawing, sculpture, engraving, and many other techniques to produce visual representations of landscapes, the human form, religious and historical events, and countless other subjects. The artistic impulse also finds expression in glass, jewelry, and new forms inspired by new technology. Indeed, judging by humanity's prolific artistic output throughout history, one must conclude that the compulsion to produce art is an inherent aspect of being human, and the results are among humanity's greatest cultural achievements: masterpieces such as the architectural marvels of ancient Greece, Michelangelo's perfectly rendered statue of *David*, Vincent van Gogh's visionary painting *Starry Night*, and endless other treasures.

The creative impulse serves many purposes for society. At its most basic level, art is a form of entertainment or the means for a satisfying or pleasant aesthetic experience. But art's true power lies not in its potential to entertain and delight but in its ability to enlighten, to reveal the truth, and by doing so to uplift the human spirit and transform the human race.

One of the primary functions of art has been to serve religion. For most of Western history, for example, artists were paid by the church to produce works with religious themes and subjects. Art was thus a tool to help human beings transcend mundane, secular reality and achieve spiritual enlightenment. One of the best-known, and largest-scale, examples of Christian religious art is the Sistine Chapel in the Vatican in Rome. In 1508 Pope Julius II commissioned Italian Renaissance artist Michelangelo to paint the chapel's vaulted ceiling, an area of 640 square yards (535 sq. m). Michelangelo spent four years on scaffolding, his neck craned, creating a panoramic fresco of some three hundred human figures. His paintings depict Old Testament prophets and heroes, sibyls of Greek mythology, and nine scenes from the Book of Genesis, including the Creation of Adam, the Fall of Adam and Eve from the Garden of Eden, and the Flood. The ceiling of the Sistine Chapel is considered one of the greatest works of Western art and has inspired the awe of countless Christian pilgrims and other religious seekers. As eighteenth-century German poet and author Johann Wolfgang von Goethe wrote, "Until you have seen this Sistine Chapel, you can have no adequate conception of what man is capable of."

In addition to inspiring religious fervor, art can serve as a force for social change. Artists are among the visionaries of any culture. As such, they often perceive injustice and wrongdoing and confront others by reflecting what they see in their work. One classic example of art as social commentary was created in May 1937, during the brutal Spanish civil war. On May 1 Spanish artist Pablo Picasso learned of the recent attack on the small Basque village of Guernica by German airplanes allied with fascist forces led by Francisco Franco. The German pilots had used the village for target practice, a three-hour bombing that killed sixteen hundred civilians. Picasso, living in Paris, channeled his outrage over the massacre into his painting *Guernica*, a black, white, and gray mural that depicts dismembered animals and fractured human figures whose faces are contorted in agonized expressions. Initially, critics and the public condemned the painting as an incoherent hodgepodge, but the work soon came to be seen as a powerful antiwar statement and remains an iconic symbol of the violence and terror that dominated world events during the remainder of the twentieth century.

The impulse to create art—whether painting animals with crude pigments on a cave wall, sculpting a human form from marble, or commemorating human tragedy in a mural—thus serves many purposes. It offers an entertaining diversion, nourishes the imagination and the spirit, decorates and beautifies the world, and chronicles the age. But underlying all these functions is the desire to reveal that which is obscure—to illuminate, clarify, and perhaps ennoble. As Picasso himself stated, "The purpose of art is washing the dust of daily life off our souls."

The Eye on Art series is intended to assist readers in understanding the various roles of art in society. Each volume offers an in-depth exploration of a major artistic movement, medium, figure, or profession. All books in this series are beautifully illustrated with full-color photographs and diagrams. Riveting narrative, clear technical explanation, informative sidebars, fully documented quotes, a bibliography, and a thorough index all provide excellent starting points for research and discussion. With these features, the Eye on Art series is a useful introduction to the world of art—a world that can offer both insight and inspiration.

Introduction

Pictures Speak the Most Universal Language

Beginning with cave paintings that sequentially depicted animals running, artists have always tried to capture movement in their work. It took the invention of the motion picture camera in the late 1800s for artists to truly achieve their goal. By making successive drawings of an action and projecting photographs of the drawings onto a screen at a continuous rate, artists could create the illusion of movement. This was the start of a new art form known as animation.

Early animation was crude. Animated figures lacked depth, detail, and realistic anatomy. Animators were not concerned with the way figures actually moved or with telling a story. Animated films focused on putting over a joke or a gag that took advantage of the character's unreality. Animated figures typically stretched and fell apart; then the film was reversed and the figures shrunk and went back together. The films were short, and lacked color or sound. The realism, depth, beauty, and engrossing stories of modern animation had their beginnings in the mind of Walt Disney. He was the first person to add sound and color to animated films, and he created the first full-length animated movie. His animated films told actual stories, and his characters had personality and charm. Disney earned a total of twenty-six Academy Awards for his work, the most of any person ever. Fifteen of them were for his animated films. According to Disney animators Frank Thomas and Ollie Johnston, "Walt's idea . . . went far beyond gags; he sought the new, the novel, the unexpected, the beautiful, and the colorful situation with warmth. Instead of thinking of cartoon material as being 'entertaining,' one might find a better concept in the word 'captivating.' Audiences had to be impressed, absorbed, involved, taken out of themselves, made to forget their own worlds and lose themselves in ours for a cartoon to succeed."[1]

For Walt Disney, animation was both a form of entertainment and a new and ever-changing form of art. As animation historian John Canemaker explains:

> It's hard to imagine the world of animation without Walt Disney. His contribution was extraordinary, actually changing the whole direction of animation in a way that probably would not have occurred without him. He was a visionary. . . . He extended the emotional borders of animation. He made animation that could compete on a social and psychological level with that of live action. . . . At the same time he kept emphasizing that animation was a different art form.[2]

Disney's work is probably better known than that of any other artist in history. The beauty and universal themes of his animated films spoke to people all over the world. "Of all of our inventions for mass communication," Disney said, "pictures still speak the most universal language."[3]

"If You Can Dream It, You Can Do It"

Creating beloved animated movies is only part of Walt Disney's accomplishments. There are few artists who have had as strong an impact on popular culture as Disney. His imagination and creativity have had a lasting influence on everything from

filmmaking and entertainment to urban planning and education. In his live-action films, for instance, he originated the concept of family entertainment. That is films without unnecessary violence, sexuality, or foul language; films, he hoped, that adults and children could enjoy together. And he took family entertainment to new levels in creating Disneyland, the world's first theme park.

Disney also pioneered television programming and documentary filmmaking. He was the first person to marry entertainment and education, crafting entertaining documentaries and educational films, for which he won a total of nine Academy Awards. He helped develop stereophonic surround sound, and brought classical music to animation. He pioneered the field of animatronics, a form of three-dimensional animation; was involved in urban planning and the development of a model city; and was instrumental in the creation of the California Institute of the Arts, a college dedicated to integrating visual and performing arts. Throughout his life, Disney was always trying to innovate and create new things. "It's kind of fun to do the impossible," he told a reporter. "If you can dream it, you can do it."[4]

A Hard Climb

Disney's accomplishments are all the more amazing considering the struggles he faced. He was a self-made man, making his way with talent, hard work, imagination, and determination. He grew up in poverty, never finished high school, and had little art or filmmaking training. Most of what he knew was self-taught. Always modest and down-to-earth, he never claimed to be a genius or a great artist. And even though he ran a huge studio and was world famous, he insisted everyone call him Walt rather than Mr. Disney.

Throughout his life, he repeatedly faced financial ruin. But he never let a lack of money discourage him. Stubborn and optimistic, when he believed in an idea, he would risk everything for it. When he did have a success, he was reluctant to repeat it. "You can't top pigs with pigs,"[5] he told movie theater owners

A statue at Walt Disney World's Magic Kingdom in Lake Buena Vista, Florida, shows Disney with his most famous creation, Mickey Mouse.

when they asked him to make a sequel to his animated film *The Three Little Pigs*. Instead, he insisted on trying something new despite the risk and the widespread skepticism his innovations elicited. He was called a fool when he tried to add sound to cartoons, when he decided to make a full-length animated movie, when he used color, when he went into television, and when he created Disneyland. He never let any of this deter him.

A Lasting Legacy

More than four decades after his death, Disney's legacy lives on. His theme parks are a model for family entertainment throughout the world. The beautiful artwork used in his films has been exhibited in museums and has served as an inspiration for graphic artists, children's book illustrators, and animators all over the globe. This group includes Osamu Tezuka, the father of

Japanese anime; children's book author and illustrator Maurice Sendak; and John Lasseter, the creator of animated films like *Toy Story*, *A Bug's Life*, and *Cars*, to name a few.

Disney's animated films continue to bring pleasure to millions of people. His decades-old films still attract huge audiences to movie theaters and sell millions of DVDs. His animated characters have influenced toy-making, educational material, interior decor, music, jewelry, and fashion design. In truth, it is hard to imagine a world without Disney's contributions. As Joseph Titizian, a cast member at Disneyland wrote: "Walt lives in our hearts and minds today, even for those of us who were born after his death."[6]

It All Began with Mickey

Walter Elias Disney was born in Chicago, Illinois, on December 5, 1901, to Elias and Flora Disney. He had three older brothers and a younger sister. The family moved around a lot as Elias struggled to support his family. When Walt was four years old, the family moved to a farm in Marceline, Missouri. Walt was very happy there. Disney's memories of Marceline remained with him all his life. He modeled Disneyland's Main Street after Marceline. And the animals that populate Disney's animated features had their origins on the family farm.

The Young Artist

Right from the start Walt loved to draw. Marceline was the site of one of his earliest artistic endeavors. He and his sister Ruth painted a mural on the side of the family house with tar. As his sister recalled:

> Walt and I were left there alone. We spied a big barrel of tar and opened it up. . . . Walt said, "Oh, this would be real good to paint with." . . . So we went to work on

The Walt Disney Hometown Museum, housed in a 1913 train depot in Marceline, Missouri, attracts Disney fans to see the place where he was raised.

the long side of the white house, the side that faced the main road. He drew houses. I remember, with smoke coming out of them. . . . My father was so angry that he just left it there. It was still there on the side of the house when we moved.[7]

"I Loved This Drawing Business"

In 1911, the bank foreclosed on the farm. The family, minus the two oldest boys, Herbert and Raymond, who had already left home, moved to Kansas City, Missouri. There, Elias became a newspaper distributor. Walt and his brother Roy delivered newspapers for him. Each boy delivered three hundred newspapers at dawn and again at dusk. When Roy left home in 1912, Walt took over his route, too.

When Walt had a spare moment, he drew caricatures, humorous drawings that exaggerate a person's or animal's features in a well-meaning, fun way. In exchange for free haircuts, he made caricatures of the men who hung out at the local barbershop. To entertain his sister, he made a little book with a series of drawings that seemed to move when he flipped the pages. That was his first attempt at animation.

Whenever he had money, he went to vaudeville shows and movies. He loved the silly skits and silent films. Soon, he was creating his own skits, which he wrote, directed, starred in, and made the scenery, costumes, and props for, combining what would become his two great loves—art and entertainment. "I was quite a ham," he recalled. "I loved this drawing business. . . . When I put on a stage play I would make my own scenery."[8]

Charlie Chaplin, shown performing in a 1918 film, was one of the great film-makers and comedy stars of the silent film era. The young Walt Disney was greatly influenced by vaudeville and silent films.

A HARD WORKER

Walt Disney grew up in poverty. His father was a stern man with a bad temper who beat his children. He had a strong work ethic, which he passed down to his children. They often worked for him, but he never paid them.

One of Walt's earliest jobs was delivering newspapers for his father. Walt got up at 4:30 a.m. and loaded three hundred papers onto a wooden cart, which he pushed from house to house. His father insisted that Walt put the newspapers behind each subscriber's storm door, so Walt could not just toss the paper, but had to climb up and down stairs. He often trudged through snowdrifts to make his deliveries, and had nightmares all his life about skipping a customer. He also delivered evening papers.

Before dropping out of school, Walt sold snacks on passenger trains during school breaks. After dropping out, he sorted mail in the post office in the morning, emptied city mailboxes in the afternoon, and loaded freight onto trains at night. Walt never minded working hard.

In 1917, the family moved again, this time back to Chicago. There, Elias managed a jelly factory, where Walt worked at night. During the day, he attended high school, serving as the cartoonist for the school newspaper. On Saturdays, he took art classes at the Chicago Academy of Fine Arts. This was his only formal art training. At home, he compiled a gag file filled with jokes for cartoons, and worked late into the night sketching.

Walt dropped out of high school in 1918. His family needed money, and he preferred working to school. He held down three jobs simultaneously. At the time, World War I was going on. Walt tried to enlist, but was too young to serve. The Red Cross, however, accepted him as an ambulance driver. Walt arrived in Paris, France, in December 1918, a month after the war ended. Instead of transporting wounded soldiers, he carried supplies to French villages. Walt's ambulance was easy to recognize. He decorated it with original cartoons. In his spare time, he made caricatures of the remaining troops and he drew political cartoons, which he sent to magazines in the states. They were all rejected.

Experimenting with Animation

Returning to the United States in the fall of 1919, Disney settled in Kansas City, where he lived with his brothers Roy and Herbert. They urged him to apply for a job at a local bank that was hiring tellers. But he wanted to draw. A commercial art company hired him to draw pictures of farm animals and equipment for a farm supply catalog. He became friends with a co-worker named Ub Iwerks (pronounced Uhb I-werks). The two had not been employed long when they were laid off. Disney suggested they start their own commercial art company; quite an endeavor for two teenage artists. They had only been in business a month when they were offered jobs at Kansas City Film Ad, a company that made one-minute animated commercials for movie theaters. The idea of making moving pictures excited the two artists and they took the jobs, abandoning their fledging business.

At Kansas City Film Ad, Disney created cutout paper figures of people and animals with movable joints. He pinned the figures to a sheet and gave them to a cameraman with an outline of the action. The cameraman used an early animation technique known as stop motion to create the illusion of movement. This involved incrementally changing the position of the figure's movable part in each film frame. When the frames were played in sequence, the figure appeared to be moving. For instance, a knee could be gradually raised and lowered creating the impression of marching. Disney recalled: "They were very crude things . . . sort of little puppet things. We didn't draw

UB IWERKS

Walt Disney called Ub Iwerks the greatest animator in the world. Iwerks co-created Mickey Mouse with Walt. He drew the first three Mickey Mouse cartoons practically on his own, and was the fastest animator in the business, producing as many as seven hundred pictures a day. Today the average animator produces about one hundred drawings a week!

Iwerks and Disney met when they were both seventeen years old. They worked together until 1930, when Iwerks started his own animation studio. Iwerks created two cartoon series on his own—*Flip the Frog* and *Willy Whooper*. Neither was a success.

In 1940, he returned to the Disney studio. He eventually became the head of research and development, where he developed new processes for photography and new animation tools. He became an expert in developing special visual effects and was responsible for some of the most remarkable special visual effects in Disney films. He also created the special visual effects for the Alfred Hitchcock movie *The Birds*.

Iwerks died in 1971. He was a technical genius in the field of animation and special visual effects. He was honored as a Disney Legend by the Walt Disney Company in 1989.

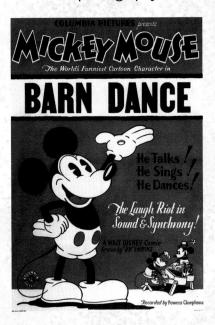

"Drawn by Ub Iwerks" is among the information included in this publicity poster for a 1929 Mickey Mouse cartoon.

An illustrator works with a cel—a sheet of transparent celluloid used in cartoon animation—in her studio in 1943. Disney began experimenting with cels early in his career.

them like we do today. I used to make little cut-away things and joints were pinned and we put them under the camera and we'd maneuver them and make them do things."[9]

Disney was fascinated by the animation process. He watched the cameramen as they photographed the figures. Soon, he could operate the camera. Wanting to learn more, he checked out two books from the library, which he carefully studied. One was a book on animal and human locomotion. The other was *Animated Cartoons: How They Are Made, Their Origin and Development*, by Edwin G. Lutz. Disney told an interviewer: "It was just something the guy put together to make a buck. But, still, there are ideas in there."[10]

The idea that Disney found most intriguing was using transparent celluloid sheets known as cels to make animated films. In this process, artists draw a series of pictures onto cels, each slightly different from the next. For instance, the position of a character's arms and legs can be changed slightly on each cel. The drawings are outlined in ink and the solid areas are painted black. Next, the cels are layered on top of each other. The composite image is photographed over a pre-drawn static background with movie film. The film is projected onto a screen, producing the illusion of movement. It takes twelve cels and twenty-four frames of film to create one second of animation. This method produced better-quality cartoons than those made with cutouts. It was used by animators in New York City which was the center of animation at that time.

Disney bought some celluloid sheets, borrowed a camera from Film Ad, set up a makeshift studio in his brother Herbert's garage, and began experimenting. He filmed family members in live action, manipulated the film to create gags, then re-created the live action in cartoon form. His niece Dorothy recalls: "He had me stroll down the walk in front of the house carrying a full milk bottle. . . . I pretended to accidentally break the bottle, spilling the milk over everything. And then he reversed the film so that I backed up and the milk came back up into the bottle."[11]

Disney decided to try selling his creations, which he called Laugh-O-Grams. When a local movie theater owner asked Disney for a price, he blurted out a figure that was exactly what it cost to make the films, forgetting an important element—a profit. Disney never cared about money. It was simply a means to an end. He needed it to pay for his experiments.

The first Laugh-O-Gram debuted on March 29, 1921. It was a one-minute program filler. Disney agreed to make one per week. He bought a movie camera and rented a little shop, where he made the films at night after working all day. It was a lot to do alone. He advertised for boys who wanted to learn cartooning to help him. Soon he had three unpaid assistants.

Making his own cartoons let Disney be more creative than his work at Film Ad. Disney decided to quit his job and turn his experiments into a full-time business, Laugh-O-Grams Inc. He found a few local investors, convinced Iwerks to join him, and signed a contract with Pictorial Clubs, a film distributor. At twenty years old, Disney was the president of his own company. As president, he did most of the animation, operated the camera, and washed the cels so they could be reused. Laugh-O-

Grams produced six cartoons. The artwork was primitive and the animation jerky, but the gags were clever. Unfortunately, Pictorial Clubs went out of business without ever paying Disney.

That was the beginning of the end for Laugh-O-Grams Inc. Disney's brothers had left Kansas City. Disney was living in a boardinghouse. Unable to pay his rent, he slept on the floor of the Laugh-O-Grams office, showered at the train station, and ate cold beans from a can. "I was all alone," he said years later. "It was lonesome. . . . I was so . . . hungry."[12]

Mixing Animation and Live Action

By 1923, Laugh-O-Grams was bankrupt. Disney decided to move to Los Angeles, California, where Roy and his uncle Robert lived. He tried to get a job making live-action movies, but no one wanted to hire him. At Roy's urging, Walt went back to cartooning. Once again he set up a makeshift studio, this time in his uncle's garage. Believing he could not compete with the cartoons coming out of New York, he turned to an innovative idea he had been working on in Kansas City—combining live action and animation. Animator Max Fleischer had made *Out of the Inkwell*, a cartoon series in which animated figures jump off the drawing board and interact with humans. Disney decided to reverse the process and have a real little girl enter an animated world where she had adventures. He called the series *Alice Comedies*. The films were ten minutes long, silent, and in black and white.

Disney sent Margaret Winkler, a New York film distributor, a sample reel, and she offered him a contract for six *Alice* films. Disney was ecstatic. It was a chance to start an animation studio again, and Roy would be his partner. The brothers were a perfect match. Practical Roy would run the business, while Walt created the films. With money Roy borrowed, Walt bought a secondhand movie camera, rented a work space that they called Disney Brothers Studio (and later changed to the Walt Disney Company), and started making the *Alice* films.

Disney finished the first *Alice* comedy, *Alice's Day at Sea*, in December 1923. He wrote the script, came up with all the gags, did all the animation, washed the cels, directed six-year-old Virginia Davis to play Alice, and did most of the filming. He hired two women to ink and paint the cels. One of these employees was a young woman named Lillian Bounds, whom Disney called Lilly, and whom he married in 1925.

Disney completed six *Alice* comedies practically by himself. The films typically opened and closed with a brief live-action scene framing an animated dream sequence. The animation was the primary focus of the films. With the success of the films, Disney hired some of his Laugh-O-Grams animators, including Ub Iwerks, to assist him, and he rented a bigger building to work in. He had so much to do producing new *Alice* films that he gradually started to draw less. As a producer, he came up with gags and stories, supervised the animators' and photographers' work, and edited the films. He acted out every story and every movement for the animators before they started drawing, and then checked their work before it was photographed. According to Frank Thomas and Ollie Johnston:

> Walt could animate as well as any of the men working on the *Alice* series . . . but none of them seemed to have his wealth of ideas or knowledge of how a piece of business should be presented. This gradually caused him to give up his own drawing board to concentrate on the areas of his greatest talents. At one point, he set up a table in the middle of the animators' room and had them bring their scenes to him when they were done. Studying the action, Walt called for new drawings where necessary and timed the scenes so they would be most effective. He corrected staging and expressions and was quick to educate those working with him.[13]

Disney made fifty-six *Alice* films. With each film, he tried to make the animation smoother and the gags funnier. But by 1927, he was eager to try something different—an animated series named *Oswald the Lucky Rabbit*. Ten years later, it would inspire *Bugs Bunny*, created by animator Leon Schlesinger.

Oswald the Lucky Rabbit

Oswald was a solid black rabbit with a white face. Animator Otto Messmer, the creator of *Felix the Cat*, one of the most popular cartoon series of the time, had discovered that a solid black object was more distinct and moved better on the screen than a line drawing. Therefore, Disney made Oswald solid black. Although Disney did not do the actual animation for the series, he wrote scenarios for each scene, accompanied by sketches showing the animators how to stage the action. He insisted on quality, refusing to use cost-cutting methods like cycles, an animation technique in which a series of drawings are repeated over and over.

The series was very popular. A reviewer for *Motion Picture News* described the series as "chock full of humor" and predicted, "This series is bound to be popular . . . if the present standard is maintained."[14]

Maintaining a high standard was expensive, and the studio was not making money. In 1928, Disney and Lilly went to New York to ask the distributor for more money. Although Roy handled finances, in the early years Disney often dealt with the distributor. The distributor was Margaret Winkler's husband, Charles Mintz. Not only did Mintz refuse to pay more for the cartoons, he announced that his company owned the copyright for the *Oswald* character. This meant Disney could not use the character in his films without Mintz's approval. Mintz wanted Disney to shut down his studio and work directly for him. If Disney refused, he would lose *Oswald*, and almost all of his animators, whom Mintz had already hired. A furious Disney refused.

The Birth of Mickey Mouse

Before heading back to California, Walt sent Roy a telegram: "Arrive home Sunday. . . . Don't worry. Everything OK."[15] But

DRAWING MICKEY MOUSE

An eight-minute Mickey Mouse cartoon consists of about eighty-five hundred drawings. In order to produce Mickey Mouse cartoons quickly with a limited staff, Walt Disney and collaborator Ub Iwerks tried to make Mickey Mouse as simple a figure as possible. As Disney explained:

*M*ickey had to be simple. We had to push out seven hundred feet of film every two weeks. His head was a circle with an oblong circle for a snout. The ears were also circles so they could be drawn the same, no matter how he turned his head. His body was like a pear, and he had a long tail. His legs were pipe stems, and we stuck them in large shoes to give him the look of a kid wearing his father's shoes. We didn't want him to have mouse hands because he was supposed to be more human. So we gave him gloves. Five fingers seemed like too much on such a little figure, so we took away one. That was one less finger to animate. To provide a little detail, we gave him the two-button pants. There was no mouse hair, or any other frills that would slow down the animation.

Quoted in Bob Thomas. *Disney's Art of Animation: From Mickey Mouse to Beauty and the Beast.* New York: Hyperion, 1991, p. 12.

everything was not okay. Disney's hard work had been stolen from him. Without the *Oswald* series, the studio had no income, but it did have debt. Disney had recently purchased land on which to build a bigger studio. Unless Disney came up with a successful new series, his second animation studio would go bankrupt. Ever upbeat, on the train trip back to California, he made sketch after sketch of possible cartoon characters to replace Oswald. He came up with a mouse that he named Mortimer. Lilly did not like that name. "I think he should be called Mickey

Mouse,"[16] she declared. And there, on a train somewhere in the middle of America, Mickey Mouse was born.

When Disney got back to the studio, Ub Iwerks was the only animator remaining. The two old friends went to work making Mickey Mouse cartoons. Iwerks did the drawings based on Disney's design and Disney came up with the stories. Lilly and Roy's wife, Edna, inked and painted the cels. From the start, Disney tried to make Mickey endearing. He gave him human-like qualities such as a can-do, optimistic, adventurous personality (not unlike Walt's) that he felt audiences would relate to. This was a new concept in cartoons. As he explained: "We wanted something appealing, and we thought of a tiny bit of a mouse . . . a little fellow trying to do the best he could. . . . When people laugh at Mickey Mouse, it's because he's so human; and that is the secret of his popularity."[17]

Disney and Iwerks completed three Mickey Mouse cartoons. Disney could not find a distributor for them. Facing disaster, he came up with what was considered a crazy idea at the time—adding sound to the third cartoon, *Steamboat Willie*. In 1927, *The Jazz Singer*, the first movie with sound, was released. Many people in the movie business thought sound was a passing fad. Disney was convinced that sound was the future of movies. "Sound effects and talking pictures are more than mere novelty," he told Roy at the time. "They are here to stay and in time will develop into a wonderful thing. The ones who get in on the ground floor are the ones that will more likely profit by its future development. That is, providing they work for quality and not quantity and quick money."[18]

Convinced that sound would save the studio, Disney sold his car and mortgaged his house in order to finance his experiment. Adding sound to a cartoon had never been done before. The sound had to match the action of the cartoon frame by frame. Disney, who had no musical education, had to figure out how to make it work. He developed a method that was later adopted by the animation industry. He used a metronome to count the number of beats per minute in a piece of music. Next he calculated how many film frames were needed to match the music.

Then he made marks on the film to synchronize the musical beats to the animation. He took the marked film to New York in search of someone with recording equipment. Experts advised him to record the sound on a vinyl phonograph record, which movie theater projectionists could play with the cartoon. It was the least expensive method, but Disney did not like the idea. The record could skip or break. He was convinced the only way to synchronize the sound and action was to record the sound directly on the film. He hired a man named Pat Powers, who owned a recording system, to help him. Disney also hired

A publicity shot from 1935 that combines photography and cartoon drawing shows Walt Disney and Mickey Mouse.

musicians and a conductor to add music and sound effects to the film. The first attempt was a costly failure. The conductor refused to follow Disney's cue marks on the film and the music and animation were out of sync. The second attempt was better. To save money, Disney provided Mickey's squeaks, Mickey's girlfriend Minnie Mouse's squeals, and the voice of a parrot shouting, "Man overboard." In future cartoons, Disney supplied Mickey's high, squeaky voice. He had a special connection with the character. In fact, many of Disney's animators insisted that Mickey Mouse was Walt's alter ego. According to animator John Hench: "Walt's relationship with Mickey was hard to miss. In a way, he was the personification of Walt. . . . I don't think Walt felt quite the same about any of the other characters as he did about Mickey."[19]

Steamboat Willie debuted on November 18, 1928. Nothing like it had ever been seen before. Mickey Mouse became an international sensation. By the end of 1931, a total of thirty-six Mickey Mouse cartoons had been released. The Mickey Mouse fan club had more than 1 million members all over the world, and merchandise with the Mickey Mouse logo, including watches, toy trains, and ice cream cones, was selling like crazy. The success of Mickey Mouse saved the Walt Disney studio. "It all began with Mickey," Disney told an interviewer years later, "and I am eternally grateful to him."[20]

A New Art Form

Combining animation with sound put Walt Disney on the cutting edge of animation technology. Hiring more animators, he worked tirelessly to improve each new *Mickey Mouse* cartoon. He lived and breathed animation, working all day, then prowling the studio at night inspecting the work on the animators' desks. In his spare time, he went to movie theaters to study competitors' cartoons.

He came up with new characters. Mickey and Minnie were joined by Pluto the dim-witted dog, Horace the horse, Clarabelle the cow, and later Goofy and Donald Duck. Their humanlike foibles made them instantaneous hits with the public.

Innovative Techniques

After Mickey Mouse's success, animators flocked to Disney's studio, located in the Silver Lake district of Los Angeles, California. It was fast replacing New York as the center of animation. The addition of new talent made Disney set higher and higher standards. Although he no longer did any animation, he was deeply involved in every step of the filmmaking process. He came up with most of the stories and gags, coordinated

Some of Walt Disney's most enduring characters—Pluto, Goofy, Mickey Mouse, Minnie Mouse, and Donald Duck (left to right)—pose with Walt's nephew Roy O. Disney at a Hollywood Walk of Fame ceremony.

the sound and music, and closely supervised his animators and challenged them to keep improving. Disney initially portrayed each character for the animators, and acted out every sound, voice, story, gag, movement, and facial expression before they started drawing. According to Disney animator Dick Huemer, "Walt would take stories and act them out at a meeting; kill you laughing they were so funny. . . . And there it would be. You'd have a feeling of the whole thing. You'd know exactly what he wanted."[21]

To help the team of animators, Disney came up with a number of innovations that became standard elements in making animated films. One, the storyboard, is used in live-action films as well.

Animation is a visual medium. It is difficult to describe the artwork that goes into making an animated film. A storyboard, which is simply a corkboard on which drawings are attached in sequence, allows animators to tell a complete story through sketches. It helps organize a developing cartoon. Before Disney created the storyboard, chaos reigned. As Disney recalled:

We would sit in [animator Webb Smith's] office in the morning and think up gags. . . . After lunch I'd drop in Webb's office and he'd have the sequence sketched out on sheets of paper. They'd be scattered all over the room, on desks, on the floor, every place. It got tough to follow them; we decided to pin all the sketches on the wall in sequence. That was the first storyboard.[22]

Roughs, In-Betweeners, and Pencil Tests

Rough drawings, in-betweeners, and pencil tests were other advances that Disney and his artists came up with to help improve their art. Disney believed that animation was a new evolving art form. It was an animator's job to capture and re-create movement. Disney felt that to get the best results, animators had to work differently than traditional artists. Traditional artists work on the same picture from start to finish, adding details, retouching, and perfecting their work. According to Disney, when animators worked this way, their work was too stiff. They spent too much time on little details and not enough on portraying movement. To rectify this, Disney had the animators do rough drawings focusing on movement, which often looked more like swirls of tangled lines than cartoon characters. The animators turned these drawings over to assistants known as in-betweeners, or clean-up men, who added the details. Drawing roughly helped the animators be freer and more creative, and it added liveliness and stronger movement to the animation.

After the in-betweeners refined the drawings, they photographed them on a filmstrip. Gathering in a small room known as the sweatbox, groups of animators, supervised by Disney, reviewed the film by running it through a small projector before it was transferred to cels. This was known as a pencil test. As the group watched the pencil test, they brainstormed, making comments and corrections. Although Disney was the boss, he encouraged the animators to speak their mind and would often

ANIMATION PIONEERS

Walt Disney was an animation pioneer. Other animators who came before him influenced his work. Winsor McCay was one of the earliest. He was probably the first person to consider animation an art form. Between 1911 and 1921, he produced a number of animated films. His most famous is *Gertie the Dinosaur*. Gertie was the first animated figure to have a personality. She showed shyness and wept huge tears. Although McCay's films are considered animation classics today, they were not commercially successful. To make a living, McCay gave up animation and worked for a newspaper instead.

After McCay, animators did not try to give their characters personality or emotion until Walt Disney. Animated cartoons were based on silly gags and ridiculous situations. *Felix the Cat*, a popular cartoon series created by Otto Messmer, which first appeared in 1919, came the closest to having a character with some personality. Messmer said he was inspired by McCay. But the cartoons largely depended on visual tricks. Nevertheless, Felix was the first cartoon star and the first to have licensed merchandise, paving the way for Mickey Mouse.

go with the majority opinion. "We just get together the bunch of us, and work things out," he told a reporter in 1929. "We voice our opinions and sometimes we have good old-fashioned scraps but in the end things get ironed out and we have something we're all proud of."[23]

One of Disney's greatest skills was motivating and coordinating all the people at his studio to bring his visions to life. As he told a reporter in 1956, "The vital part I played is coordinating these talents. And encouraging these talents. . . . I have an organization over there of people who are really specialists. You can't match them anywhere in the world for what they can do. But they all need to be pulled together."[24]

By working with the animators and encouraging them to help each other, Disney created an atmosphere where creativity was applauded and every one learned from each other. This encouraged experimentation and innovation. The results were finer and finer cartoons.

Silly Symphonies

As his animators became more skillful, Disney wanted to try new things. He did not want his studio to be identified with only one cartoon series. Disney got the idea for a series of short cartoons without continuing characters based on musical compositions. He called them *Silly Symphonies*. At first the cartoons in the series were more like animated poems than traditional

Walt Disney tries to persuade a penguin to perform for a segment of the *Silly Symphonies* series in 1934.

cartoons. They had no story line, moving from one musical scene and comic dance routine to another. The concept freed Disney from the restrictions of traditional cartoons and let him explore a more artistic kind of animation, with an emphasis on fluid movement, sound, and atmosphere rather than gags. According to film historians J.B. Kaufman and Russell Merritt, "The *Silly Symphonies* followed Mickey by less than a year, but it was mainly because of them that critics were describing Walt Disney not only as a pioneer, but also as a popular entertainer working at the margins of serious art."[25]

The first cartoon in the series, *The Skeleton Dance*, was a graveyard frolic that combined music, humor, and a scary atmosphere. It was the first animated film to set a mood. The film opened with flashes of lightning set against a solid black background, followed by a close-up of pulsing circles that turn out to be the eyes of an owl. The owl is perched on a tree in which the moving branches transform into skinny arms and fingers. There are vampire bats, a huge furry spider, snarling black cats, and a dog that howls at the moon. Skeletons with rubbery limbs jump out of the graves, use bones to play music on each other's ribs, then form a chorus line and comically dance to spooky music. What is especially amazing is how Disney and his staff managed to get the skeletons' movements to mirror the music, a feat that no other animation studio could achieve at that time.

When the cartoon was completed, Disney expected Pat Powers, who had become the distributor of the *Mickey Mouse* cartoons, to place it in movie theaters. Powers was not interested. He wanted more *Mickey Mouse* cartoons. Walt believed the film would be a hit. He convinced the manager of a movie theater in Hollywood to show it. Sure enough, Disney was right. The audience loved it, and the *Silly Symphonies* series was launched.

Business Problems

Between 1929 and 1939, Disney produced seventy-five *Silly Symphonies*. He won seven Academy Awards for the cartoons, and the series led to other studios making similar films, includ-

Disney's innovative four-layer camera, seen here in a photo from 1953, gave cartoons the illusion of depth.

ing Warner Brothers' *Looney Tunes*. The series became a way for Disney to experiment with animation, sound, and special effects, which would be essential for producing full-length animated features in the future. As the series progressed, Disney added plots and more dramatic story lines to some cartoons. He added small and large innovations that made the animated characters seem more realistic and made the action flow more elegantly. Among other innovations, he experimented with animating special effects, shooting with more-modern cameras, using real backgrounds rather than hand-drawn ones, and using overlapping action, a new animation technique created at the studio, which gave the illusion that parts of a character's body continued to move after the other parts of the figure came to rest.

All of these innovations, combined with Disney's insistence on quality, were expensive. One *Silly Symphony* required fifteen thousand handmade drawings, each of which had to be inked and painted. Any refinement in technique or new technology increased the cost. Although the series was a big hit, between Disney's spending and Pat Powers taking a huge portion of the proceeds, the studio was once again in financial trouble. According to Frank Thomas and Ollie Johnston:

> Walt was constantly plagued by money problems and by distributors who took the lion's share of the tiny profit from his creative efforts. He always felt that the way to win the battle was to "beat them with product," to make films so good that the world would beat a path to his door. . . . The important thing was to improve the product because audiences would respond to a better film. He did not believe in cutting corners to save money if it hurt the quality, nor would he turn out a cheap product just to make money. Instead of looking for the maximum profit, he was looking for the maximum audience response.[26]

In need of money, first Roy, then Walt, went to the distributor. Like Charles Mintz, Pat Powers refused to help. So the Walt Disney Company broke its contract with Powers. But Powers did not walk away empty-handed. The studio continued paying him for sound equipment he had provided. Worse still, Powers offered Ub Iwerks his own studio, which Iwerks accepted. There had been friction between Iwerks and Disney, because Iwerks refused to work with in-betweeners. Still, the two had been a team since they were teenagers. They created the *Alice Comedies*, *Oswald*, and *Mickey Mouse* together. Walt was stunned by his friend's decision. It took him years to get over the loss. But he did not hold a grudge. Ten years later when Iwerks needed a job, Disney welcomed him back.

Experimenting with Color

Faced with limited income and rising costs, Roy tried to institute money-saving practices at the studio, which did not go over well with Walt. He thought the best way to bring in more money was to improve his cartoons, this time by adding color—something that had never been done before.

Disney had been unsuccessfully experimenting with chemicals, trying to add color to his cartoons for a few years. In the early 1930s, the Technicolor Motion Picture Company developed a process of making color film by combining the primary colors on three strips of film negatives. The method was not perfected, and would not be used in live-action movies until 1935 in the film *Becky Sharp*, but Disney wanted to try it on his cartoons.

It was a risky proposition. Adding color would triple the cost of making a single cartoon, and it might be a total failure. Roy argued that the studio's new distributor, United Artists, would not advance more money for color, and there was a good chance that colored paint would not stick to the cels the way black paint did. Disney would not take no for an answer. Color, he felt, would make cartoons more exciting and move the art of animation forward. He made a deal with Technicolor that granted the studio exclusive use of the Technicolor process for two years, which barred other studios from using the process. Then he set to work.

He stopped work on *Flowers and Trees*, a half-finished *Silly Symphony*, and had his artists wash the black paint off the cels and repaint them in color. As Roy predicted, the dried colored paint chipped off the cels and faded under the light from the camera. Disney and his staff worked around the clock to develop a new type of paint that would not chip or fade. But there were other problems, too. Before the use of color, it was easy to distinguish a solid black character against a white background. Colored characters, on the other hand, had to be coordinated with the background. For example, a bluebird in a blue sky would disappear, while clashing colors such as an orange figure against a red background would not please the eye. Disney solved this problem by using bright colors for the characters and gray tones such as

HOW COLOR CHANGED ANIMATION

Adding color to animated films helped raise animation as an art form. It allowed artists to depict characters more realistically, produce elegant backgrounds, and set a mood. Disney animators Ollie Johnston and Frank Thomas explain this in their book The Illusion of Life:

Even the brightest pigments on a painting can reflect back to the viewer only a limited amount of light. Their apparent brightness is relative to itself, a range from dark to light of about 20 to 1. But with the light intensity of the projection lamp and a highly reflective screen, this brightness factor increases to an exciting 200 to 1—ten times as great! Just as the stained glass window had brought dazzling brilliance after centuries of relative dull frescoes, the introduction of light behind the film made whole new ranges of color available to the artist. Add to this the potential for building color relationships in sequence for stronger emotional response, and the artist had before him an incredible medium of self-expression.

Frank Thomas and Ollie Johnston. *The Illusion of Life*. New York: Walt Disney Productions, 1981, p. 15.

gray-blues and gray-greens in the backgrounds. "Look out a window and you will see there is gray in everything—the trees, the sky, the mountains," explains Disney artist Art Riley. "By painting our backgrounds with overtones of gray, we can make the scenes look natural and allow the animated figures to be legible."[27]

There was also the question about how intense the colors should be. Some of the animators wanted to mute the colors, but Disney insisted on making them bright. Audiences had never seen a colored cartoon before. Disney reasoned that bright colors would impress them. He was right. *Flowers and Trees* debuted in 1932, and was an overnight sensation. Every step of the way, Disney was pioneering and inventing, going where no artist had gone before. His experiment paid off. In 1932, Disney was awarded an Academy Award for *Flowers and Trees*, the first ever for an animated film. The excitement the film generated brought money back into the studio's empty coffers, allowing Disney to keep moving forward.

The Three Little Pigs

Disney's next challenge was to combine color and sound with appealing characters. He had already created a likable character in Mickey Mouse, but his goal was to make his characters more and more charming and give them more human-like traits. In *The Three Little Pigs*, an eight-minute *Silly Symphony* that premiered in 1933, Disney created what was probably his most appealing characters to date, and combined them with a simple but captivating plot and a clever use of color, music,

The three voice actors in the center—Dorothy Compton, Pinto Colvig, and Mary Moder (left to right)—spoke and sang as all of the characters and created the sound effects for *The Three Little Pigs and the Big Bad Wolf*. Walt Disney is on the left, and Frank Churchill, who wrote and played the score, is at right.

and sound. In fact, it was the first animated film to produce a hit song, "Who's Afraid of the Big Bad Wolf." With the Great Depression going on, the song became an anthem of hope and determination for millions of financially strapped Americans. The cartoon was originally conceived without a song. Disney felt there was something missing. He maintained that it needed a catchy jingle-like song to help the story along. Frank Churchill, a studio musician, came up with the tune.

In addition to the song, other elements of the film were quite inventive, such as the way Disney used art, sound, and movement to develop each pig's character. For instance, the two playful pigs wear silly sailor suits and childish hats. They sing in high falsetto voices and dance little jigs. One plays a flute and the other a fiddle, while the hardworking pig wears overalls and talks his song in a serious voice.

Disney also started thinking more about backgrounds and design and how these could support the characters' personalities. He had the background artists add pictures of sports figures and pretty female pigs to the walls of the first two pigs' houses, while the third pig had dour pictures of his mother and father. This, too, was a new concept. It would pave the way for the incredible detail in the background of *Pinocchio* six years later.

As usual, Disney was involved in every aspect of the film. It took him months to adapt the popular folktale into a story suitable for the screen. He insisted that the story have heart and warmth, that in the end good triumph over evil, and that the pig that worked the hardest be rewarded. These were beliefs that defined Disney's life and struck a chord with viewers. When the film premiered, it was an enormous hit. It became so popular that movie theaters billed it over the main feature on their marquees and ran the film for months.

New Additions

Around the time *The Three Little Pigs* premiered, many new things were happening in Walt Disney's life. Both the studio and Disney's family were expanding. The studio now had more

Walt Disney did not live the life of a rich celebrity. He was a modest man who rarely attended big Hollywood parties, preferring to spend time with his family. He doted on his daughters, Diane and Sharon. Disney drove them to school every day and attended all of their school events. When he came home from work, he roughhoused with the girls.

The family ate dinner together every night. Disney often described the stories he was working on during the meal, entertaining his family with funny voices and facial expressions. On weekends, he took the girls to amusement parks or on other family outings, and Walt and Lilly often hosted barbecues for the animators and their families. Disney's large home, with its big lawn and swimming pool, was a perfect place for all the children to play. Disney spent hours in the pool with his daughters. He taught them how to swim. When they were older, he taught them to horseback ride and to drive.

The girls never thought of their father as a celebrity. To them, he was dad.

Walt Disney and his family, en route to England, wave to onlookers from the deck of the ocean liner RMS *Queen Elizabeth I* in June 1949.

than one hundred artists, all of whom Disney supervised. And Disney's daughter Diane was born in 1933. Four years later, Disney and Lilly adopted their youngest daughter, Sharon. During this time period, Disney was busily exploring new animation techniques and developing new characters. Donald Duck made his debut in a *Silly Symphony* titled *The Wise Little Hen* in 1934. Disney got the idea for the duck and his distinct voice from a radio show in which a comedian imitated animal voices. Audiences loved the bad-tempered duck, and he became a regular cast member in the *Mickey Mouse* cartoons.

Donald Duck, a character who has delighted audiences since 1934, was honored with a star on the Hollywood Walk of Fame in 2004 for "achievement in film."

Learning Together

When Donald Duck made his first appearance, he had a long bill and an angular body. Disney had his artists shorten the bill and round out Donald's body in order to make him more expressive, cuddly, and easier to animate. Just as Disney and his staff reworked Donald Duck's appearance until they got it right, in each new *Mickey Mouse* cartoon and *Silly Symphony*, Disney and his staff explored and tried new things. Disney wanted his animated characters to move in the way real people and animals do. He wanted facial expressions and body language to reflect feelings. And he wanted the backgrounds to have an old-world storybook quality.

Disney and his animators were largely self-taught. The methods they used were those that cartoonists had been using for years. Although they had come far, they lacked the artistic training and technical skill to capture Disney's vision. "To do the things I wanted to do, I needed better artists," Disney explained. "A cartoonist is not the same as an artist. A cartoonist knows the shortcuts and tricks—how to do things in a hurry. His work might have been comic, but it wasn't convincing."[28] So Disney established an art school at the studio.

Disney hired Don Graham, a top art instructor at the Chouinard Art Institute in Los Angeles, California. Graham brought in prints of famous paintings for the animators to analyze. They discussed each painting's composition and use of color. Graham conducted life-drawing classes. Disney felt the animators needed to learn to draw realistically before exaggerating their drawings to suit the medium. Disney also invited guest speakers like architect Frank Lloyd Wright to lecture on art and inspiration, and writers like H.G. Wells to talk about stories. As animator Mel Shaw recalled: "Walt was really imbuing [filling] all of us with something that made us feel we were part of a movement that could be considered a Renaissance in the animated cartoon business."[29]

Disney knew there were elements of animation that could not be found in traditional art curricula. Whereas traditional art is static, animation focuses on movement. He wanted his animators to learn about timing, creating special effects, and portraying action-reaction realistically. He had them study live-action films of people and animals in motion. And he created a department in the studio in which specialty artists made three-dimensional models of characters for the animators to sketch from. He also had his animators teach classes to each other.

No other studio offered its artists this type of training and encouragement. Disney was looking to the future. He saw animation as an evolving art form, which he dreamed of taking to new levels. "Animation developed because of Walt's insistence and supervision," animator Les Clark maintains. "The animator had to wrestle with the problem of how to make the drawings work properly, but without Walt's drive it is doubtful that any of them would have tried so hard or learned what to do."[30]

A Caricature of Life

Walt Disney was eager to put his animators' new skills to use. As an artist, he was excited about the possibilities he saw in the evolving medium of animation. For a while now, he had wanted to make a full-length animated film. No one had ever done so. Animated films served as short features that were shown before the main feature. The general consensus of the movie industry was that audiences would not sit through a full-length cartoon. Indeed, when word got out about what Disney was doing, the project became known as Disney's Folly. Everyone predicted failure. Even Roy and Lilly were against the idea. Disney estimated it would cost $500,000 to make the movie—twenty times more than a *Silly Symphony*—and the movie ended up costing three times the estimate. That was money the studio would have to borrow. It was highly unlikely that the film would make back the money.

Disney did not care about the cost. As an artist, he wanted to be free of the restrictions that making an eight-minute cartoon posed. Making a full-length film would allow Disney to create a fully developed story with realistic characters that had the depth and impact of a live-action film.

Disney chose the fairy tale *Snow White* for the film. He had seen a silent movie of *Snow White* when he was a boy and never

The Disney Brothers Studio started in 1923 in a small office. Since then, the physical plant has grown tremendously. In 1925, Disney bought land on Hyperion Avenue in Los Angeles for a larger studio. By 1937, Disney had outgrown the Hyperion studio. It was replaced by a larger, state-of-the-art studio on fifty-one acres in Burbank, California. Walt Disney helped design the new studio, which resembles a college campus. In the center is the animation building. It is surrounded by the ink and paint building and the camera buildings, where the artwork is completed and photographed; the cutting building, where the films are edited; the sound building; and the special visual effects building. The buildings are linked by underground tunnels, making it easy to go from one to the other in bad weather.

There are three sound stages where live-action movies are shot, and a back lot designed for filming Western movies. There is also a machine shop, where many of the rides used at Disneyland were designed and built; and a model shop where molds, casts, and fiberglass figures are made. The campus also includes a large theater used to screen films.

Dwarfs from the Disney version of *Snow White* appear to hold up one of the buildings in the sprawling Walt Disney Studios complex in Burbank, California.

forgot it. In Disney's view, it had all the elements of a good story—romance, comedy, an evil villain, and a happy ending in which good triumphs over evil—and it was well-suited to animation. Despite the naysayers, Disney's mind was made up. He was making the film.

Snow White and the Seven Dwarfs

Disney's animators first heard about his plan in 1934, when he gathered them together and began telling them the story of *Snow White* as he envisioned it. He acted out every scene, stooping down to impersonate the dwarfs, cocking an eyebrow diabolically as he pretended to be the evil queen. He described the colors, the backgrounds, the music, and the forest creatures. The performance took two hours. By the time Disney finished, everyone was as excited as he about the possibilities.

Making the film was a challenge. Disney wanted each character to have a distinct personality, and to move and show emotion just like real actors. He felt this was the only way that the audience would connect with the characters. He called this a caricature of life. "Our most important aim is to develop definite personalities in our cartoon characters," he told a reporter in 1938. "We invest them with life by endowing them with human weaknesses which we exaggerate in a humorous way. Rather than a caricature of individuals, our work is a caricature of life. In *Snow White* was an illustration of what I mean. There were the parent birds consumed with pride over their offspring's singing. Suddenly, he hit a sour note and their wincing

An animator works with a series of cels for Disney's 1937 version of *Snow White and the Seven Dwarfs,* the company's first full-length animated feature.

showed their humiliation. It was funny because it resolved human reactions into caricature."[31]

Some characters were easier to work with than others. Because animals show their emotions through actions, the forest animals were simplest. As Disney explained: "You know why the animals dominate animated cartoons? It's because their reaction to any kind of stimulus is expressed physically. Often the entire body comes into play. Take a joyful dog. His tail wags, his torso wiggles, his ears flop."[32]

Depicting human emotions was trickier. Humans are more inhibited than animals. Disney studied people. He realized that humans show emotions in subtle ways, that language has anatomy, and that facial and body movements emphasize feeling. For instance, lowered eyes show embarrassment, clearing the throat nervousness, and a clinched jaw anger. The animators used this concept to make the characters seem more realistic and to evoke an emotional reaction from the audience.

Portraying Snow White's movements was also difficult. Disney and his staff did not have a lot of experience portraying young women. Audiences knew how humans moved. If Disney and his animators could not depict human movement realistically, the audience would not relate to the character. After rejecting drawing after drawing, Disney got the idea of filming a live actress portraying Snow White. The animators used the actress' movements as a guide. Then, because Disney wanted Snow White to move with more grace and beauty than an actual person, they exaggerated the movements. This method worked so well that Disney used it in all his future animated films. He explained:

> The animator couldn't think up everything. Even such a simple matter as rising from a chair is important. In the old days, a cartoon figure would simply rise to an erect position and walk away. But that isn't how people move. By studying live-action film, the animators could see that the figure leaned forward in the chair, placed his hands on the arms and pushed himself into a standing position. The important thing is to use live

THE ANIMATION PROCESS

$\mathcal{M}$aking a full-length, hand-drawn animated film is complicated. At its most basic, it involves the following process:

1. Animators, story people, and directors create a storyboard, which lays out the story.
2. The dialogue is recorded.
3. Animators make rough drawings. In-betweeners refine the drawings. The drawings are pencil tested.
4. Inkers transfer the drawings to cels.
5. Painters paint colors on the back of the cels, so they do not blur the inked outline on the front.
6. Backgrounds are painted on cels or on glass.
7. The cels are layered on top of the background and photographed. A special camera with a lens mounted facing down is used.
8. Once all the drawings are filmed, the dialogue is added.
9. The film is edited.
10. Copies, or prints, are made of the film, and it is released to theaters.

action as a guide and not as a crutch. When we first started using it, some animators tried to copy the live action exactly. Their work was stilted. . . . The fact is that humans can't move as freely and as gracefully and comically as we can make animated figures move.[33]

The dwarfs posed other problems. In the original fairy tale they were minor figures. In Disney's vision they were integral to the story, adding humor and evoking sympathy. To make the audience relate to them, Disney insisted that each dwarf be portrayed as an easily recognizable individual with his own personality and mannerisms. Developing each character took a lot of time. Disney and the animators first came up with names for the dwarfs, which helped determine their personalities and facial expressions. Depicting their movements was also difficult. Disney modeled different walks—from waddles to bowlegged ambles—for the animators, until the group settled on one.

Disney was in the center of everything. He approved every single drawing and story change. He felt like he was creating live people, and he instilled this feeling in his animators. When the characters were fully developed, he became concerned with the filming. He wanted the movie to have the same depth as a live-action film. A standard animation camera portrays backgrounds as flat, and cannot capture perspective. This was acceptable in a short cartoon, but not in a full-length film. Disney worked with his technical staff to develop a multi-plane camera. It photographs a number of pieces of artwork at various speeds and at various distances to create a feeling of depth. With it, Disney created long shots and close-ups. He made backgrounds and foregrounds move in opposite directions. In one scene, for example, he has the evil queen drink a potion while the background spins behind her. The results were beautiful, and the camera has since become standard equipment in making animated films.

It took three years and more than 2 million drawings to complete the film. When it premiered in December 1937, the theater audience gave it a standing ovation. Disney felt vindicated. For too long, animated films were looked down on by both the film industry and the art world. Disney proved that animated films were truly art and that they could evoke the same allegiance to characters as the best live-action films. For his efforts, he received an honorary Academy Award, which consisted of one full-sized statue and seven miniatures. The citation read: "For *Snow White and the Seven Dwarfs*, recognized as a significant screen innovation which has charmed millions and pioneered a great new entertainment field."[34] That same year, Harvard and Yale Universities gave him honorary degrees. And New York's Metropolitan Museum of Art exhibited a painted still from the film; something that had never been done before. The museum credited the work to Walt Disney, but Disney had the credit changed to Walt Disney and staff.

In its first year, *Snow White and the Seven Dwarfs* earned $8 million, more than any film up until that time. More importantly, it set the standard for every animated film that came after it. As animation historian Charles Solomon explains: "We're still seeing animated features as musicals because Snow White was a musical. The idea that these should be based on fairy tales comes directly from Snow White. The kind of storytelling you see in Snow White is still the goal aspired to by animators. Snow White is one of the watersheds in the history of animation."[35]

A Drawing Factory

Once *Snow White* was finished, Disney was ready for new challenges. He hired five hundred more artists, and began work on three new full-length features: *Pinocchio, Fantasia,* and *Bambi.* The staff now included animators, background artists, inkers, painters, model makers, color experts, special effects people, writers or story men, sound experts, musicians, and cameramen. At the same time, the Disney brothers began construction of a larger studio on fifty acres in Burbank, California, which Disney helped design.

Gifted artists were everywhere. Model department artist Martin Provensen called the studio a drawing factory. "Drawing," he said, "was everywhere; the walls were plastered with drawings. You developed a certain attitude towards drawing: You saw drawing as a way of talking, and a way of feeling."[36]

Among the most talented were nine animators who became Disney's right-hand men. Although they were young, Disney dubbed them the Nine Old Men, as a joke after the name President Franklin D. Roosevelt gave to the nine justices of the Supreme Court. Working closely with each other and with

THE "NINE OLD MEN"

Disney's so-called Nine Old Men created many famous characters and moments in Disney films, and trained hundreds of other animators. The nine were:

Les Clark (1907–1979). He worked at the studio for forty-eight years. He took over drawing Mickey Mouse after Ub Iwerks left.

Marc Davis (1913–2000). Davis was known for his animated female characters, including Tinker Bell and Cruella De Vil, and his work as an Imagineer. He helped create Disneyland.

Ollie Johnston (1912–2008). Johnston was an expert at animating feelings and friendships, including Baloo and Mowgli from *The Jungle Book*, and the three fairies in *Sleeping Beauty*.

Milt Kahl (1909–2002). He was an expert at capturing human characters. His characters include Peter Pan and Alice of *Alice in Wonderland*.

Ward Kimball (1914–2008). His specialty was wacky characters like The Mad Hatter.

Eric Larson (1905–1988). He trained many young animators after Walt Disney's death.

John Lounsberry (1911–1976). Lounsberry created loose characters, like the dancing alligator in *Fantasia*.

Wolfgang Reitherman (1909–1985). His specialty was action sequences, like the dinosaur battle in *Fantasia*.

Frank Thomas (1912–2004). He instilled emotions and personality in animated characters. He was also known for his villains, including Captain Hook.

Disney for more than twenty-five years, these men helped Disney realize his dreams. They loved animation and had total faith in Disney. Two of the Nine Old Men, Frank Thomas and Ollie Johnston, recall: "[Walt's] ideas were the best. Many times we could not understand what he wanted, but never did we lose confidence in him or his ability. We could question his judgment or his emphasis, or the way he went about achieving a result, but it was with the knowledge that Walt's way always was a very good way."[37]

Pinocchio

Lead by Disney, these young artists set to work on *Pinocchio*, a tale about a puppet without a conscience. The 1883 novel by Carlo Collodi, with its many adventures, seemed perfect for animation. But as the work progressed, Disney became increasingly dissatisfied. One of the biggest problems was the character of Pinocchio. As a marionette, he lacked humanity. He looked and moved like a wooden figure. And lacking a conscience, he committed bad deeds without remorse. Disney did not think audiences would care about the character. His solution was to change Pinocchio's appearance, making him softer, rounder, and more like a little boy. And he gave him a conscience in the form of Jiminy Cricket. At first, the animators designed Jiminy to look like an insect, but Walt did not find this appealing. He wanted him to look more like a wise little man. As animator Ward Kimball explained: "Walt said he looked too much like an insect. . . . So, he ended up not being an insect. We finally ended up with a little man. He was cute. His head is an egg. He had no ears—that's the only thing you could construe as cricket-like. . . . Walt wouldn't necessarily create the character, but he would tell you when he liked it. He did that always. He wasn't drawing. But he was giving us input."[38] Disney was spot-on. Jiminy Cricket unified the story, and became a beloved Disney character.

Charming characters were not enough. Disney wanted the film to have great atmosphere, beautiful backgrounds, and

Walt Disney (left) works with an animator on drawings of Jiminy Cricket, for the feature animated film *Pinocchio* in 1939.

a feeling of depth. Working with Disney, the color experts, background painters, and special effects animators developed new techniques to make flat areas seem more rounded, such as delicately spraying paint on the cels with an airbrush. This technique was used on the kitten in the film, making him look soft and fluffy. The multi-plane camera, too, contributed to the film's depth and beauty. More than twelve planes, or levels, on the camera were used in the opening scene, which pans over the rooftops of the quaint village, creating a more intricate view than had been seen in any live-action film of the time.

Pinocchio is considered by many animation experts to be Disney's finest work. However, it was not a commercial success.

The start of World War II in Europe in 1939 wiped out about half of Disney's market, and the film, which cost an unheard of $2.6 million to make, lost more than $1 million.

Fantasia

At the same time Disney was working on *Pinocchio*, he was producing a *Silly Symphony* starring Mickey Mouse. It was based on the story of *The Sorcerer's Apprentice*, a fairy tale about a magician's assistant who misuses his master's magical powers. The tale had been made into a concert piece by the composer Paul Dukas. Disney heard the music at a concert and was inspired to create a film done as a pantomime set to the music. While Disney was working on it, he ran into Leopold Stokowski, the conductor of the Philadelphia Symphony Orchestra. When Disney told Stokowski about the film, Stokowski volunteered to conduct the musical score. Stokowski so enjoyed working with Disney that he suggested that the two collaborate on an anthology of classical music interpreted with animation. Disney was enchanted with the idea. From this came *Fantasia*, a full-length movie consisting of eighteen beautifully illustrated classical music pieces.

Disney felt that every piece of music evoked a mood, images, movement, and colors. With this in mind, he and his animators listened to the different pieces of music and let their imaginations soar. For example, they depicted Ludwig van Beethoven's *Pastoral Symphony* with frolicking mythical forest creatures, Amilcare Ponchielli's *Dance of the Hours* with dancing hippos and ostriches, and Igor Stravinski's *Rite of Spring* with battling dinosaurs.

Fantasia was probably the most innovative and original film Disney ever made. Pairing classical music with animation had never been done before. For Disney, making *Fantasia* was a chance to expand the boundaries of what an animated film could be in terms of color, art, music, sound, design, and cultural level. "We shouldn't be thinking of this as just a cartoon," he instructed his staff. "We have worlds to conquer here."[39]

The music for the film was performed by the Philadelphia Symphony Orchestra and recorded at Philadelphia's Academy of Music. When the recorded music was played back, Disney was dissatisfied. It did not sound as rich or full as the live orchestra. Disney worked with his sound experts to develop a new kind of sound system that recorded music through multiple microphones, then played it back through multiple speakers. It was an early version of stereophonic sound, which Disney called Fantasound. But not many audiences heard it, because only a handful of movie theaters were willing to purchase the expensive Fantasound equipment.

Fantasia cost Disney $2.2 million to make, and that was just the start. Walt's plan was to add to it constantly, creating new sequences and deleting old ones so that it would be a constantly

Fantasia—one of Disney's most innovative films and the first movie to pair classical music with cartoons—includes a segment in which Mickey Mouse plays a wizard.

evolving work of art. However, with the war in Europe eliminating a huge market for the film, Disney once again lost money and he could not continue his experiment. If he had done so, it is likely that animated films might have become more abstract and focus less on telling a story and more on color, design, and music.

Bambi

Despite these financial losses, Disney continued work on *Bambi*. It was the most challenging of the three films and the last to be released. It was the first animated film to deal seriously with death, and Disney obsessed over the story. His greatest concern was the scene in which Bambi's mother dies. The story men suggested a graphic scene in which Bambi discovers his mother's bloody corpse, but Disney went in another direction. He had Bambi call for his mother without the audience seeing her body. He felt that showing Bambi's emotions would touch the audience's heart in a more profound manner than showing the dead deer. He was right. That scene has since become one of the most memorable and heartrending in the history of animated films.

Disney also had original ideas for the animation and special effects. He wanted the animals to look much more realistic than had ever been done before. According to Ollie Johnston, who helped animate the film: "We'd never done an animal with anatomy before, and Walt wanted the deer to have personality and be believable."[40]

Disney set up a zoo at the studio with live fawns, rabbits, owls, and skunks so that the animators could study the animals' anatomy and movements. In addition, he had the model department construct tiny models of the animals. The animators traced the model of Bambi's father in order to get consistent drawings of the volume and perspective of the stag's antlers as he moved. Disney also brought in hundreds of animal photographs and films of animals in their natural habitat for the animators to study.

Walt Disney sketches a pair of fawns in 1938 as part of preparatory studies for his 1942 film *Bambi*.

Disney also wanted the forest to mirror an actual forest. To make this happen, he had the animators and background artists study photographs of forests, focusing on details like the texture of tree bark or the veins in a leaf, which they replicated in their artwork. He was also concerned with depicting the change of seasons in the forest realistically, and used different music and colors to portray each season. He had the same concerns for the animated special effects. If they were not presented realistically, the movie would not be convincing. Natural occurrences like rain, snow, and fire are difficult to portray realistically. Disney and his special effects team went to work experimenting on ways to depict these events. They discovered that filming drops of water falling in slow motion against a dark background and superimposing the film on the animation was more convincing than drawing raindrops. They depicted snow in the same manner, using bleached cornflakes rather than water droplets. They also experimented with rubbing colored gels on the camera's lens, blurring the camera's focus, and filming through frosted glass.

The final result was a gorgeous, deeply touching, realistic film. In fact, some critics complained it was too realistic. *Bambi* premiered in 1942, just months after the United States entered World War II. People were not going to the movies, and *Bambi*, like *Fantasia* and *Pinocchio*, was a huge financial failure. Yet, despite the fact that these films were not immediate money-makers, over time they would make the studio millions of dollars.

Snow White and the Seven Dwarfs, *Pinocchio*, *Fantasia*, and *Bambi* are still viewed by audiences today. They were the collaborative work of many artists, but without Walt Disney's vision, these films would have never been created. As Disney explained:

> I have had a stubborn, blind confidence in the cartoon medium, a determination to show the skeptics that the animated cartoon was deserving of a better place; that it was more than a mere "filler" on the program; that it was more than a novelty; that it could be one of the greatest mediums of fantasy and entertainment yet developed.[41]

In making these films, Disney proved his point. He created works of art that helped refine and advance the art of animation and set the standard for animation today.

Many Mediums

By 1942, the studio was $4.5 million in debt. To ease the problem, in April 1940, brothers Walt and Roy Disney took the company public. That is, they sold stock in the company. This helped, but it did not completely pay off the huge debt.

The Strike

It was obvious to the people who worked at the studio that the business was in financial trouble. By the spring of 1941, some employees' salaries had been cut and about a hundred people had been laid off. Rumors of massive layoffs abounded.

Many of the studio's workers were already represented by various unions. The animators, however, were not unionized. With rumors flowing freely, Herbert Sorrell, an organizer with the American Federation of Labor (AFL), a large national labor union, targeted the animators. Some of the animators wanted to join Sorrell's union, while others favored the Federation of Screen Cartoonists, an independent local union. Because the animators seemed split, Disney proposed they vote to decide which union they wanted to represent them. Sorrell insisted a vote was unnecessary. He threatened to shut down the studio unless Disney signed with his union. Because he did not have the support of all of Disney's employees, Sorrell planned to do this by organizing a secondary strike at Technicolor. Striking Technicolor would stop Disney from getting the film it needed to make movies. Disney described what happened:

> This fellow Sorrell came in and said I have your artists. . . . You sign with me or I'll strike you. I said there's only one thing I can do. I've got to live with these boys. I've got to have a vote through the labor board and whatever way it comes out I go. Then, I'm keeping

During the Disney Studios animator strike of 1941, a picketer holds a sign that implies wages at the studio were comparable to pay in fast food jobs.

faith with them. I'm not signing with you on your say so. He said, "I can make a dust bowl of your place" and he did everything to smear me.[42]

Sorrell did not wait for a vote. On May 29, 1941, he called a strike. Disney was shocked to see a picket line around the studio. Forty percent of the animators walked out. Sorrell also launched a bitter media campaign against Disney, portraying him as a rich man who exploited labor. Taking their cue from Sorrell, some of the strikers made inflammatory remarks about Disney from the picket line.

Disney took the strike personally. He was close to many of the animators. Throughout the years, he tried to make their workplace pleasant with noon volleyball games, free snacks, specially designed furniture, and flexible work hours. He felt they were like a family, and he was the father who looked after them. According to Disney's daughter Diane, "The strike was incomprehensible to him, where it came from, the virulence of it."[43] Many of the animators, however, felt differently. They often worked overtime without additional pay, and their pay structure was disorganized. Individual animators received extra pay based on Disney's opinion of their skill. Some were highly paid, while many others were paid poorly.

Beyond being hurt, the strike affected Disney's politics. He was convinced the strike was inspired by Communists. As a result, Disney became more politically conservative and anti-Communist for the rest of his life.

The Latin American Tour

While the strike was going on, President Franklin Roosevelt asked Disney to represent the United States on a goodwill tour of Latin America. At the time, Germany was trying to get the nations of Latin America to ally themselves with the Axis Powers (the group of countries led by Germany, Italy, and Japan that opposed the Allied Powers, led by Great Britain, France, the Soviet Union, and the United States, during World War II).

Disney films on a beach in Rio de Janeiro, Brazil, during a 1941 tour of Latin America.

Disney's work was very popular in Latin America. Roosevelt hoped that sending Disney to Latin America would keep the nations he visited from supporting the Nazis. Disney agreed to go if he could work while he was there. On August 17, 1941, Walt, his wife Lilly, and eighteen artists chosen by Disney took off for a trip that included stops in Brazil, Argentina, Chile, Uruguay, Bolivia, Peru, and Mexico.

Disney was greeted by large crowds wherever he went. He and the group attended state dinners; met Latin American artists, filmmakers, and musicians; went to nightclubs, barbecues, and festivals; visited beaches and parks; and took a boat ride down the Amazon River. The latter inspired Disneyland's Jungle Cruise ride years later.

Throughout the trip, Disney filmed everything he saw with a sixteen-millimeter motion picture camera, while the artists sketched. While Disney was in Uruguay, he got word that his father had died. His mother had died tragically four years earlier when a leaky furnace that was giving off carbon monoxide caused her death by asphyxiation. He was upset about his father's death, but remained in South America as planned.

When the group returned to the studio in October, the animators were unionized under the American Federation of Labor and the strike was over. They turned their work into two films, *Saludos Amigos* and *The Three Caballeros*. The films combined Disney's live footage, which showcased Latin America's modern cities and sophisticated people, with colorful animation and music. The films delighted both North and South American audiences and improved relations between the continents. According to film historian Alfred Charles Richard Jr., the films "did more to cement a community of interest between peoples of the Americas in a few months than the State Department had in fifty years."[44]

War Comes to the Studio

Disney's involvement with the government and the war effort was just beginning. On December 7, 1941, the day the Japanese bombed Pearl Harbor, the United States Army commandeered Disney's studio to house seven hundred troops. They remained there for eight months. For the rest of the war, the armed forces had free run of the studio. They used the sound stages and parking sheds to repair trucks and weapons and store ammunition.

Disney shelved his plans to make three new animated features, *Cinderella*, *Peter Pan*, and *Alice in Wonderland*, and turned his attention to helping the war effort by making animated training films for the military. The films, which featured characters like Goofy and Donald Duck, covered everything from how to identify enemy aircraft to how to prevent disease. Presenting complex information in an entertaining and enlightening manner excited Disney. Making these films sparked his future interest in making educational films for children.

Disney also created propaganda films for the government. He worked as hard on these as on any of his cartoon features. One, starring Donald Duck, encouraged Americans to help the war effort by paying their taxes. It was so successful that the number of Americans paying their taxes increased by 37 percent.

Donald Duck also starred in the film *Der Fuehrer's Face* (originally titled *Donald Duck in Nutziland*). In it, Donald has a nightmare that he is forced to work in a Nazi munitions factory, where he must salute Nazi leader Adolf Hitler constantly. The film is accompanied by a song in which each salute is punctuated by a contemptuous raspberry sound. It ends with a caricature of Hitler's face pummeled by ripe tomatoes. The silly cartoon so infuriated Hitler that he banned it, and Donald Duck, too. But the Nazis could not control the film's spread. It was translated into multiple languages and smuggled into occupied European countries, where it delighted audiences. Disney won an Academy Award for the cartoon.

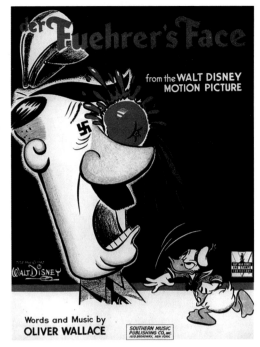

Donald Duck throws a tomato at German dictator Adolf Hitler on the cover of the sheet music for the 1942 Disney film *Der Fuehrer's Face.*

The payments Disney received for his wartime work did not cover his expenses. Some of his work was never paid for. For instance, he and his staff designed twelve hundred different character insignia emblems for military units, which Disney paid for personally. For Disney, supporting the war effort was a matter of patriotism and respect for the troops. "I had to do it," Disney explained. "Those kids grew up on Mickey Mouse. I owed it to 'em."[45]

A Bear Coming Out of Hibernation

When the war ended in 1945, the studio was in even worse debt than it had been before the war. "We were like a bear coming out of hibernation, with no fat on us,"[46] Roy Disney recalled. Disney was eager to start work on *Cinderella*, *Peter Pan*, and *Alice in Wonderland*, no matter the cost. Roy insisted that that they did not have the money and wanted to go back

A Team of Many Artists

It took a team of many talented people collaborating with each other and with Walt Disney to bring his visions to the screen. A few of the people involved in making animated features include:

Actors: Artists who act out the scenes as a guide for the animators. They also provide the animated characters' voices.

Animators: Artists who create the actual animation.

Animated special effects artists: Artists who create animated special effects such as rain, fire, and smoke.

Background artists: Artists who create the backgrounds for the film.

Camera operators: Artists who film the movie.

Character model artists: Artists who make three-dimensional models of the characters as a guide for the animators.

Musicians: Artists who compose the music in the films.

Producers: The team that oversees the total project, coordinating all the people involved.

Story people: Writers who come up with the story for a film by looking at sketches on a storyboard.

Sound technicians: Artists who work with sound recording.

Stylists: Artists who make the drawings and paintings from which the design, color, and mood of a film emerge.

to making short cartoons. Disney, the risk taker and dreamer, was opposed to going backward. Rather than argue, the two brothers compromised. Walt put off making any full-length animated films for the time being, and between 1946 and 1948 made three packaged features, *Make Mine Music*, *Fun and Fancy Free*, and *Melody Time*, instead. These were compilations of short cartoons set to contemporary music. At the same time, using what he learned from combining live action and animation in *The Three Caballeros* and *Saludos Amigos*, Disney made *Song of the South*, a full-length feature film that mixed live drama with fanciful animation. It was based on the Uncle Remus stories written by Joel Chandler Harris, and was set in the Southern United States after the Civil War.

The film, which was 70 percent live action, was Disney's first step in the new direction he was about to follow, making live-action feature films. He was moving in this direction for a number of reasons. Live-action films cost less to make than animated films, which was important at a time when the studio had little money. And it was a new challenge, something he had never done before. As he recalled:

> I knew the diversifying of the business would be the salvation of it. I tried that in the beginning, because I didn't want to be stuck with the Mouse. So I went into the *Silly Symphonies*. It did work out. The Symphonies led to the features; without the work I did on the Symphonies, I'd never have been prepared even to tackle *Snow White*. A lot of the things I did in the Symphonies led to what I did in *Fantasia*. . . . Now I wanted to go beyond even that; I wanted to go beyond the cartoon. Because the cartoon had narrowed itself down. I could make them either seven or eight minutes long—or eighty minutes long. I tried [to] package things, where I put five or six together to make an eighty minute feature. Now I needed to diversify further, and that meant live action.[47]

Combining Technicolor, sophisticated animation, and live action was technically complex and required thorough planning. Disney filmed the live action in front of sets that were painted to look like cartoon backgrounds. After the film was edited, the animators added the cartoon characters.

The award-winning, though controversial, 1946 Disney film *Song of the South* ingeniously combined live action and animation.

Disney was as demanding of quality in the live-action portions of the film as he was of the animation. He worked as hard to develop his actors' talents as he had his animators'. Over time, he repeatedly featured many of the same actors in different films.

Song of the South premiered in 1946. It produced a hit song, "Zip-a-Dee-Doo-Dah," which won an Academy Award. The film itself was controversial. Some critics believed the film's depiction of Uncle Remus as a happy former slave was racist and diminished the horrors of slavery. This was not Disney's intention. As he explained:

> I was familiar with the Uncle Remus tales since boyhood. From the time I began making animated features I have had them definitely in my production plans. . . . And, I hope, nothing of the spirit of the earthy qual-

ity of the fables was lost. It is their timeless and living appeal; their magnificent pictorial quality; their rich and tolerant humor; their homely philosophy and cheerfulness, which made the Remus legends the top choice for our first production with flesh-and-blood players.[48]

Lights, Camera, Action

Disney's next step in preparing to make a full-length live-action feature film was making a short live-action film. After his experience making educational films during the war, Disney decided to experiment with making a short entertaining educational live-action film. He had no idea what the subject of the film would be. But because he was fascinated with America's last remaining wilderness, Alaska, he made it his focus. He sent Alfred and Elma Milotte, a husband-and-wife team of nature photographers, to Alaska to spend a year shooting film of Alaskan wildlife and native people. They had no script or outline. He directed the photographers to just sit and wait, and photograph whatever they saw. They shot 482 rolls of film, which Disney carefully studied looking for a theme. He zeroed in on the life cycle of the seals of Alaska's Pribilof Islands. He sent the team back to Alaska and instructed them to focus on the seals. He also made the decision not to show any evidence of humans such as actual people, homes, roads, or electrical poles in the film. He wanted the film to be solely about nature, and therefore timeless. Disney and his staff edited the film, which he called *Seal Island*, and set it to music. Disney's goal was to create a documentary that was simultaneously informative and entertaining. This was before the creation of IMAX films and television channels devoted to nature and animals. Indeed, these were inspired by Disney's work.

The film was the first of thirteen films known as *True-Life Adventures*. To make them, Disney sent nature photographers all over the world without pre-written material. Once he viewed their work, he came up with a theme. Eight *True-Life*

WALT DISNEY AND SALVADOR DALÍ

In 1946, Walt Disney and Spanish artist Salvador Dalí teamed up to make a short animated film known as *Destino*. Dalí was a surrealist. Surrealism is an art movement characterized by highly imaginative images. Dalí's most famous painting, *The Persistence of Memory*, portrays melting pocket watches. Dalí held Disney in high esteem. He believed that *Fantasia* was a masterpiece of surrealism, and wanted to create a surrealistic animated film with Disney.

The two men worked to turn a Mexican ballad into a six-minute animated film about love and loss. However, when the studio ran out of money, the film was scrapped. Disney and Dalí remained friends for the rest of their lives.

What remained of their collaboration were storyboards, along with drawings and paintings by Dalí. In 2003, the Disney studio finally made the film, using some of the original artwork and some computer imagery. The film has been shown in museums throughout the world, and was nominated for an Academy Award.

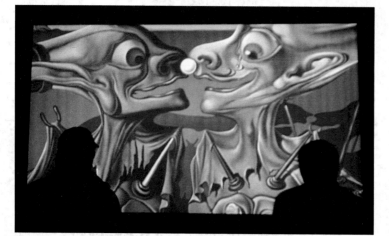

Destino, a short film by Salvador Dalí and Walt Disney, is screened at the Tate Modern gallery in London, England, in 2007.

Adventures won Academy Awards, including *Seal Island*. Other films in the series include *Beaver Valley*, *Bear Country*, and *The Living Desert*. The films were shown in movie theaters, on television, and in schools for decades. They were the earliest films to encourage the humane treatment of animals, and the preservation of nature. As Disney explained: "These films have demonstrated that facts can be as fascinating as fiction, truth as beguiling as myth, and have opened the eyes of young and old to the beauties of the outdoor world and aroused their desire to conserve priceless natural assets."[49] The impact of the films were so great that the American Society for the Prevention of Cruelty to Animals (ASPCA) awarded Disney a gold medal honoring all he had done to instill American children with a love of animals.

Treasure Island

By 1949, Disney was ready to make a full-length live-action feature film. He chose *Treasure Island*, Robert Louis Stevenson's swashbuckling novel about pirates. Before World War II, Disney's films had made a lot of money in England. When the war began, the English government froze these funds and would not let American filmmakers take their profits out of England after the war. But they could use the money in England. Disney used the frozen funds to make the film in England.

He kept control over the planning of the film by having an artist attend all the preproduction meetings in England and prepare storyboards with pencil sketches of exactly what would be photographed in each scene. These were sent to Disney in California for his approval. He pored over each one. Then he sent them back with his corrections and suggestions. Once the filming began, he took his family to England for six months so that he could supervise the production. When the filming was complete, he was heavily involved in editing it. *Treasure Island* was released in 1950. Many critics were unhappy with the film, claiming Disney made too many changes to the original book. Still, it made a modest profit at the time.

In the next few years, Disney made three more live-action adventure films in England. Unlike other live-action films that targeted either children or adults, Disney's films targeted families. His goal was to make films that adults and children could enjoy together. This concept inspired a new genre in filmmaking: family entertainment. It would characterize all of Disney's future films. Over the years, some critics called many of these movies sentimental and corny, but Disney stood by them. As he explained in 1960: "It's a natural thing for me to want to do those sorts of things. I would hate to think I'd ever do anything I didn't have a feeling for. . . . I'm kind of simple and corny at heart, and I think the majority of people are on my side."[50]

Cinderella, Alice, and Peter

Disney's success with live action helped the studio get a large loan, which let Disney turn his attention to *Cinderella*, *Alice in Wonderland*, and *Peter Pan*. The first to be released was *Cinderella*. It was just the kind of animated feature Disney did best. It was based on a fairy tale, had a sympathetic heroine, a handsome prince, a nasty villainess, funny mice, and a happy ending in which good triumphs over evil.

Disney was involved in every aspect of making the film, especially developing the story, the characters, and the soundtrack. He worked closely with Ilene Woods, the actress who provided Cinderella's voice, and came up with the idea of recording her singing, humming, and whistling on different tracks so that she could harmonize with herself as her character cleaned house. Recording sound in this manner had never been done before. As Woods recalled:

> To me, he was a true visionary. Others would say, "Can we?" And Walt would always say, "We can." And, you'd believe him, because every time he said, "We can," he did. When we were recording "Sing Sweet Nightingale," for example . . . he asked, "Ilene can you sing harmony with yourself?" I said, "Gee, Mr. Disney,

I don't know. I can't hum and whistle at the same time, but what did you have in mind?" He replied, "I can see it." And he turned to the engineer and said, "We'll put the headphones on her, and she'll sing second-part harmony. I see her scrubbing the floor when another bubble comes up and she sings third part harmony.'" The engineer sat there and said, "If you say so Walt, we can do it." It was really beautiful. The blend is unbelievable when the same person is doing all the parts.[51]

In a scene from the 1950 Disney film *Cinderella*, the poor and mistreated main character is magically dressed for a palace ball by her fairy godmother.

When the film was released in 1950, it was Disney's first full-length animated movie in eight years. The public embraced it, and it was a huge hit. *Alice in Wonderland*, which was released in 1951, was less successful. Right from the start, Disney had trouble with it. The English literary classic, written by Lewis

THE WALT DISNEY FAMILY MUSEUM

The Walt Disney Family Museum, which opened in San Francisco, California, in 2010, is dedicated to Walt Disney. Disney's daughter Diane Disney Miller started the museum after a survey showed that many young people think Walt Disney is a fictional character. The first floor of the museum displays artifacts from Disney's youth, such as the cartoons he drew in high school, a Model T ambulance like the one he drove in Europe, and Laugh-O-Gram film clips.

The second floor is reached by an elevator designed to look like the railroad car that took Walt to California in 1923. Different exhibits on the second floor present scripts, storyboards, rough and refined sketches, cels, and three-dimensional character models from Disney's animated films. There are also letters written by Disney, and early Disney merchandise like Mickey Mouse toothbrushes, tricycles, and watches. Hands-on exhibits allow museumgoers to synchronize sound effects with animation.

A multi-plane camera takes up two floors. A special hall exhibits twenty-six of Disney's Oscar trophies, as well as other awards. The museum also contains a film archive and offers lectures, concerts, film screenings, and special exhibits.

Carroll, about a girl who falls down a rabbit hole and meets weird characters, did not translate well into movie form. It did not have a structured plot, it was quite long, and it featured eighty-eight eccentric characters, none of whom were very endearing. Disney spent years trying to make the story emotionally engaging, but was never satisfied with what he came up with. To compensate, Disney made the music, artwork, and elements of fantasy the film's focal points.

Critics praised the animation and the film's brightly colored modern backgrounds. But British reviewers criticized the movie because it diverged too far from the book, while American critics thought it should have diverged more. For his part, Disney felt the movie lacked heart. Interestingly, it became a big hit when it was re-released in the 1960s. The animation and artwork were labeled psychedelic and embraced by young people experimenting with mind-altering drugs like LSD.

Disney was happier with *Peter Pan*, as were critics and movie audiences. Disney started working on adapting the novel by James Barrie in 1939. He explored many possibilities on how to tell it, and finally came up with a story he liked in 1951. The film was released in 1953. It was acclaimed for its cleverness, color, synchronization of sound to movement, and the technical artistry of the opening scene in which Peter Pan flies over London, England, and around Big Ben. To create it, Disney had the cameraman use the multi-plane camera to photograph twenty levels of artwork.

Peter Pan was the last film that Disney and all of the Nine Old Men worked on together, and the last film released through RKO, a distribution company that was not part of the Walt Disney Company. Right after the film's release, the Walt Disney Company formed Buena Vista, a Disney-owned and -operated distribution company. Other changes would occur in the next few years, too. Through it all, Walt Disney would continue innovating and moving forward. It was the path he followed all his life, and would continue to follow until his death.

A Source of Joy

Walt Disney worked ceaselessly to turn his dreams into reality. In the 1950s and 1960s, he was involved in many projects in diverse mediums, some of which had never before been explored.

"I Can Fly Again"

By 1950, television was becoming popular in the United States. People in the movie industry viewed it as a threat to movie theater attendance and refused to work in the new medium. Disney felt differently. He thought that television was a perfect medium for publicizing his films and bringing people into theaters. With that in mind, he produced a television special promoting *Alice in Wonderland* that aired on Christmas Day in 1950 and a similar Christmas program in 1952, promoting *Peter Pan*. Then, in 1954, he signed a contract with the American Broadcasting Company (ABC) to produce a weekly one-hour series. Disney had complete control of the program and retained the rights to all his work.

Everyone in the movie industry predicted failure. Theater owners threatened to boycott Disney movies if Disney went ahead with his plans, but they did not act on their threat. Disney ignored them all and trusted his instincts. He named the series *Disneyland*, after another project, a theme park, he was hoping to promote on the show. Disney hosted each show. His down-to-earth manner and the entertaining programming won over audiences. The show was a big hit.

The first show featured a tour of the studio. Other shows promoted upcoming films, or featured older Disney cartoons. But the biggest hit of the first season were three shows about the frontiersman Davy Crockett, which Disney produced just for television. Disney came up with the idea for the series and

The role of Davy Crockett turned unknown actor Fess Parker, shown in character around 1955, into a huge movie star.

carefully designed the look and format. He also did all the casting. Against the advice of his staff, he chose an unknown actor named Fess Parker for the role of Davy Crockett.

The public loved the series. The catchy theme song, which Disney had studio musician George Bruns come up with to bridge the various adventures in each program, became a number-one hit. Coonskin caps, like the one Davy Crockett wore, became the rage. Fess Parker became a megastar. Ironically, although Disney went into television to promote his films, he wound up turning the *Davy Crockett* television programs into a feature film. Television viewers flocked to theaters to see *Davy Crockett* in color.

Disney's next television venture was *The Mickey Mouse Club*, a five-day-per-week, one-hour show geared to children. It was the first quality programming for children on television, and it inspired shows like *Sesame Street* in the future. Financially, the show made no sense. It cost more to make than ABC paid for it. But Disney insisted on making it no matter the cost. He saw it as a way to entertain and educate children. The show included cartoons about health, citizenship, culture, and safety, as well as live-action serials based on children's books. The twenty-four talented children who anchored the show were called the Mouseketeers. Disney refused to use professional child actors as Mousekeeters. Instead, he cast gifted amateurs whom he worked with to develop their talent.

The Mickey Mouse Club was another smash hit. Three-quarters of the television sets in the United States tuned into the show every day. Twenty-four thousand mouse-ear caps like those worn by the Mouseketeers were sold each day. And the Mouseketeers became celebrities. Moreover, a new generation of children came to love Mickey Mouse.

At the same time, Disney started a new company called WED Enterprises, based on the initials of his name. It was a personal corporation not tied to stockholders. Under WED, Disney produced *Zorro*, a television series, based on a silent film about a masked avenger in eighteenth-century California. Disney spared no expense on the series. He helped design the

sets and spent a fortune on them in order to make them authentic. In those days, the average television program cost about $7,000 per show to make, while each half-hour-long *Zorro* cost about $82,000. Disney insisted that no one could put a price on quality or creativity, and once again, the show, which ran from 1957 to 1959, was a hit.

Disney loved working in television. The only thing missing was color. Although most people did not think it would happen, Disney predicted that color television was the next step. In 1961, he made a deal with the National Broadcasting Company (NBC) to produce *Walt Disney's Wonderful World of Color*, a series similar to *Disneyland*, but filmed in color. The show ran in various versions for decades, becoming the longest-running weekly prime-time show in history. Disney's instincts about television had been right. And he enjoyed the freedom working in the new medium gave him. "I haven't had so much fun since my early days in the business when I had the latitude to experiment," he told a reporter in 1961. "With TV, it's like a cage has been opened and I can fly again."[52]

Special Effects and More

The submarine in the film adaptation of Jules Verne's *20,000 Leagues Under the Sea* was designed by Walt Disney himself.

At the same time Disney was creating his television programs, he was producing more feature films. The live-action film *20,000 Leagues Under the Sea*, based on a science fiction novel by Jules Verne, premiered in 1954 and was the first full-length live-action movie Disney produced in the United States. In

the next decade, he followed it with other live-action dramas, including *Old Yeller*, *Swiss Family Robinson*, and *Kidnapped*; three animated features: *Lady and the Tramp*, *Sleeping Beauty*, and *101 Dalmatians*; and a very successful series of live-action family comedies, among which *The Shaggy Dog*, *The Absent-Minded Professor*, and *The Parent Trap* were the most popular. Disney achieved many firsts in these films, especially in *20,000 Leagues Under the Sea*. He worked for more than a year developing the script. As in *Zorro*, he was very involved in the set design. He insisted that the film's submarine fit Verne's description of a submarine designed as a sea monster, and that the interior of the ship reflect the time period with its lush Victorian style. His attention to the tiniest detail was most evident in the filming, especially in key underwater scenes filmed in the Caribbean Sea. Disney and his staff created specialized equipment for these scenes, including a pressurized watertight camera. One sequence, of a submerged burial, was the biggest underwater scene ever filmed. It took a crew of forty-two men wearing heavy diving gear eight days to film it.

Another scene, featuring a battle with a giant squid, was one of Disney's earliest attempts at animatronics, translating film animation to three-dimensional objects in order to give them the illusion of life. For this scene, Disney worked with his artists to create a lifelike monster that moved using hydraulics (compressed air and electronics). Disney filmed the shot in a howling storm created with special effects. This required the construction of a huge water tank, tons of water blown into a sound stage, wind machines, and specially designed lights that simulated lightning flashes. The results were astounding, and won the film two Academy Awards. The film is considered among the best science fiction films of all times. According to Steve Biodrowski, editor of the online magazine *Cinefantastique*, "*20,000 Leagues*, Disney's adaptation of Jules Verne's famous novel, is quite an achievement, a film far superior to the majority of genre efforts from the period (or any period, for that matter), with production design and technical effects that have dated hardly at all."[53]

Hands-On Hobbies

Although Disney worked long hours, he found time for a variety of hobbies, some of which provided artistic inspiration. Since childhood, Disney loved trains. As a boy, he yearned for a model train set, but his family could not afford such luxuries. In 1947, he bought his first model train set. Soon he was designing and building miniature towns for his model trains.

His next project was creating a steam-powered railroad capable of carrying passengers. It was one-eighth the size of an actual late-nineteenth-century train. Working with metal and wood, Disney designed and built each car with care. The caboose, in particular, was a work of art. Disney filled it with bunk beds, a washstand, and a pot-bellied stove that he built to scale. The train ran on a .5 mile (.80km) of track that he built outside his home. When guests visited, Disney donned an engineer's cap and took them for a ride. After one too many train wrecks, he put the train in storage, but his experience with his trains became part of his next project.

Family Park

When his daughters were little, Disney took them to an amusement park every Sunday. While his daughters rode the merry-go-round, he came up with the idea of creating a new kind of amusement park, one where people of all ages could have fun together. It would be a magical place with a variety of attractions based on Disney films and characters. There would be rides, shows, restaurants, shops, and parades, and it would be beautifully designed, clean, safe, welcoming, and easy to maneuver.

Such a park was a new concept. When Disney told people about it, they scoffed and predicted financial ruin. Not even Roy or the Walt Disney Company supported him. But Disney was keener about building the park, which he named Disneyland, than he had been about any of his former innovations. He saw it as an ever-changing work of art that he could keep developing and adding to. "Disneyland will never be completed," he said. "It

AN ANIMATED FILMOGRAPHY

Walt Disney produced 655 films. Here is a filmography of the full-length animated features he produced.

1. *Snow White and the Seven Dwarfs*, 1937.

2. *Pinocchio*, 1940.

3. *Fantasia*, 1940.

4. *Dumbo*, 1941.

5. *Bambi*, 1942.

6. *Saludos Amigos*, 1943.

7. *The Three Caballeros*, 1945.

8. *Make Mine Music*, 1946.

9. *Fun and Fancy Free*, 1947.

10. *Melody Time*, 1948.

11. *The Adventures of Icabod and Mr. Toad*, 1949.

12. *Cinderella*, 1950.

13. *Alice in Wonderland*, 1951.

14. *Peter Pan*, 1953.

15. *Lady and the Tramp*, 1955.

16. *Sleeping Beauty*, 1959.

17. *101 Dalmatians*, 1961.

18. *The Sword in the Stone*, 1963.

19. *The Jungle Book*, 1967. (Disney worked on it up until his death.)

will continue to grow as long as there is imagination left in the world."[54]

Disney borrowed on his life insurance and sold his family's vacation home to get the park started. He channeled funds from WED Enterprises into the park, and eventually got the television network ABC to loan him money for Disneyland.

Disney visited amusement parks all over the world, studying the attractions and the traffic flow. Then he and some artists with engineering skills, whom he called Imagineers, began designing the park and the attractions. Disney had a clear vision of what he wanted. Visitors would enter onto an old-timey Main Street much like the one he knew in Marceline, Missouri. Here, there would be a town square for parades, with flowers, balloons, a brass band, shops, restaurants, and theaters, and a steam engine train that circled the park. Everything in the park would be built to five-eighths scale, giving Disneyland an enchanted feeling. From Main Street, guests could head off to the four main sections of the park: Adventureland, Frontierland, Tomorrowland, and Fantasyland, where the attractions would make visitors feel like they had entered a Disney film. They could fly with Peter Pan, have a mad tea party with Alice, or explore a frontier town where Davy Crockett might have lived. To turn his ideas into reality, he described his vision to the Imagineers in the same way as he had described his films to his animators.

Walt Disney stands on the drawbridge that will become the entrance to the iconic castle at Disneyland, in Anaheim, California, during construction in 1955.

He worked on every detail of the park, from the design of the attractions to the placement of trash cans and water fountains. His years of experience as an artist and film producer helped. Just as he designed his films to flow seamlessly from scene to scene, he brought the same sense of continuity to Disneyland. He made sure that the architecture, landscaping, colors, and proportions in the different parts of the park complemented each other, and that the traffic would flow well. Speaking at Harvard University in 1963, real estate developer James Rouse called Disney's design, "The greatest piece of urban design in the United States . . . . It took an area of activity—the amusement park—and lifted it to a standard so high in its performance, in its respect for people, in its functioning for people, that it really does become a brand new thing."[55]

Disneyland, located in Anaheim, California, opened on July 15, 1955. It was an emotional day for Disney. Former Mousekeeter Sharon Baird, who was with Disney as the gates opened, recalls: "When I looked up at him, he had his hands behind his back, a grin from ear to ear, and I could see a lump in his throat and a tear streaming down his cheek."[56]

Within seven weeks, 1 million people visited Disneyland. By 2012, that number topped 500 million. Disney continued expanding and changing his creation for the rest of his life. "Disneyland," he told reporters, "is a work of love. . . . [I] hope that it will be a source of joy and inspiration to all the world."[57]

Audio-Animatronics

As Disney changed and added to Disneyland, he came up with more and more innovative attractions, such as the Enchanted Tiki Room. Disney envisioned it as a musical theater that featured dancing and singing animatronic birds and flowers. This required a new, not-yet-developed technology that combined sound and movement. Disney set the Imagineers to work on it. They came up with a system in which a magnetic sound tape and an electronic coil were placed inside animatronic figures. The tape sent signals to the coil, causing the figures to move

Walt Disney showcased his great technological and artistic skills at the 1964 World's Fair in New York City. His company created four ground-breaking audio-animatronic exhibits for the fair, including "It's a Small World" for the Pepsi-Cola pavilion.

and make sounds in sync. Disney called this system audio-animatronics. Audiences were captivated by the singing and dancing figures, and the attraction, which opened in 1963, is still at Disneyland.

From audio-animatronic birds, Disney moved to humans—specifically Abraham Lincoln. Disney created many attractions for the 1964 World's Fair in New York. One of the most memorable was Great Moments with Mr. Lincoln, which consisted of a life-size model of President Lincoln rising from a chair, walking forward, and giving a five-minute speech.

Disney went on to develop more and more sophisticated audio-animatronic figures. His work in the field provided inspiration for the many lifelike figures used in films today.

COMPUTER-ASSISTED AND COMPUTER-GENERATED ANIMATION

Throughout his life, Walt Disney embraced new technology to improve his films. In the 1990s, animators turned to computers as a way to animate films. The first full-length computer-animated film was *Toy Story*, which premiered in 1995. Today, almost all animated films are created with computers.

There are two types of computer animation—computer-assisted animation and computer-generated animation. Computer-assisted animation produces two-dimensional animation, much like hand-drawn animation. But through the use of special software and computers, animators use the computer to draw. The image is displayed on the computer screen, then changed slightly in key frames, like film frames, on the computer. Next, the computer uses a mathematical formula to fill in the movements in a process called tweening. Tweening gives the illusion of movement. Walt Disney Studios switched to computer-assisted animation in 1989.

Computer-generated animation is three-dimensional. It can produce extremely realistic virtual worlds, and is used not only in animated films, but also in video games. In this process, images are drawn on the computer, then built up using software that forms a virtual skeleton.

A Film Masterpiece

Despite all his other activities, Disney did not stop making movies. *Mary Poppins*, which debuted in 1964, is often called his masterpiece. The movie, based on a collection of stories by P.L. Travers, tells the story of a magical governess who brought a family together. It combines all the elements Disney was most famous for—animation, music, live action, special effects, and a heartwarming story. Disney got the idea for the film in the 1940s, when he read the book to his daughters. He originally planned it as a live-action film. Then, while working with Richard and Bob Sherman, who composed the music for the film, Disney got the notion of adding animation. As Richard Sherman recalled:

> I was in the middle of singing a song Bob and I just finished called "Jolly Holiday." We came to a section of the song where a quartet of waiters were going to come out and sing. . . . And then Walt said, "Waiters always remind me of penguins. I think we should have penguins as the waiters. . . . We'll animate the penguins. . . . We'll mix animation and live action. All the

In a scene from the 1964 Disney film *Mary Poppins*, Julie Andrews sings and dances with animated characters in her feature film debut.

principal players will be live action and everything else will be animation. It'll work, you'll see."[58]

The animation more than worked, as that scene, in which a live actor does a soft-shoe routine with four animated penguins, is one of the most famous dance scenes in film history. Other scenes were also remarkable. Disney came up with the idea of creating a staircase of smoke, a tea party on the ceiling, and merry-go-round horses that race through the countryside.

When the movie premiered, the audience stood up and cheered. The applause was as much for Disney himself as for the film. *Mary Poppins* went on to earn $28.5 million in its first year and won five Academy Awards. The film's success prompted worldwide attention to Disney's many achievements. He was showered with awards, including the Medal of Freedom, the United States' highest civilian honor. It was presented to Disney at the White House by President Lyndon Johnson. The citation accompanying the award read: "Artist and impresario [producer], in the course of entertaining an age, Walt Disney has created an American folklore."[59]

Reaching into the Future

Disney was not ready to rest on his laurels. Although he had little formal education, he saw a need for an institution of higher learning dedicated to the interdisciplinary study of the arts. Here, students could study fine art, drama, music, sound recording, costume design, filmmaking, photography, dance, and writing. This was the type of education that Disney believed artists working in the film industry needed.

Disney planned the school, which he named the California Institute of the Arts (CalArts), with the same dedication that he planned his films and theme park. He researched art schools and colleges throughout the country and sought the advice of college administrators; he donated land for the campus, which he helped design; he contributed $15 million of his own money; fund-raised; and set up and funded scholarships.

Disney Productions Today

The company that Walt and Roy Disney created continues to flourish. Its name remains synonymous with fine animation and family entertainment. Today it is one of the largest and most profitable global multimedia companies in the world, earning about $40 million in 2011. In addition to producing animated and live-action films, the Walt Disney Company has expanded into television, publishing, travel, theater, radio, music, online media, and consumer merchandise. Disney owns and operates the ABC television network, the Disney Channel, ESPN, A&E, and the ABC Family channel. It operates Radio Disney, and has a music division that records everything from rap music to movie soundtracks. Its travel division focuses on family travel with fourteen theme parks in North America, Europe, and Asia, resort hotels and campgrounds, and a cruise line that stops at a Caribbean island owned by Disney. The Disney publishing division produces books for adults and children, as well as comic books. Disney's theater division produces Broadway plays based on Disney films like *Beauty and the Beast* and *The Lion King*.

Disney established the school in 1961. It was the first degree-offering school for the arts in the United States. Disney felt that it was his greatest achievement. The school and the artists it nurtured would live on long after him. Today, CalArts is considered one of the finest art schools in the world.

In addition to planning CalArts, Disney was planning a larger version of Disneyland that would be built in Florida. Part of the project was the construction of the Experimental Prototype Community of Tomorrow (EPCOT), Disney's vision of a model city of the future. Disney threw himself into the project. He studied books on urban planning, and made dozens of sketches and blueprints. He was full of ideas about what the city would be like. He wanted it to be safe, clean, and quiet, showcasing new technology, and providing residents with a good quality of life. He planned the city in the shape of a circle with businesses in the center and apartment buildings surrounding the business area. Circling the apartment buildings, he planned a greenbelt with parks and lakes. Houses facing the greenbelt filled the perimeter of the circle. The city would be covered by a dome and house about twenty thousand people. Cars would operate underground, making the city pedestrian friendly, and moving walkways and a monorail would provide transportation from the houses to the city center.

Disney died before EPCOT could be built. After his death, Roy Disney continued work on the Florida theme park, which he named Walt Disney World. But the Walt Disney Company did not feel capable of running a model city. A theme park named EPCOT showcasing world cultures and innovative technology was built in its place. It embodies many of Disney's ideas and values about the future.

Final Days

Walt Disney continued working on his many projects until the day he died. In early November 1966, he was diagnosed with terminal lung cancer. He kept his illness secret from everyone but his family. Although weak and in pain, he continued going to the studio. But his condition deteriorated rapidly. He was taken to the hospital on November 30th and never came out. Yet he never stopped dreaming. The night before his death, Disney used the ceiling tiles above his hospital bed as a grid map to explain his ideas for the layout of Walt Disney World to his brother.

Walt Disney died on December 15, 1966. His body was cremated and his family held a private memorial service. The whole world grieved. When word of his death reached the studio, many employees wept openly. World leaders expressed

Notes

Introduction: Pictures Speak the Most Universal Language

1. Frank Thomas and Ollie Johnston. *The Illusion of Life*. New York: Walt Disney Productions, 1981, pp. 34–35.
2. Quoted in Katherine and Richard Greene. *Inside the Dream*. New York: Roundtable, 2001, p. 186.
3. Quoted in "Walt Disney Quotes." Just Disney. www.justdisney.com/walt _disney/quotes/quotes01.html.
4. Quoted in "Walt Disney Quotes." Brainy Quote. www.brainyquote.com /quotes/authors/w/walt_disney_2 .html.
5. Quoted in "Three Little Pigs." *The Encyclopedia of Disney Animated Shorts*. www.disneyshorts.org/shorts .aspx?shortID=187.
6. Quoted in Greene. *Inside the Dream*, p. 184.

Chapter 1: It All Began with Mickey

7. Quoted in Bob Thomas. *Walt Disney: An American Original*. New York: Simon & Schuster, 1976, pp. 28–29.
8. Quoted in Michael Barrier. *The Animated Man*. Berkeley: University of California Press, 2007, p. 21.
9. Quoted in Kathy Merlock Jackson. "Interview with Fletcher Markle." In *Walt Disney: Conversations*, edited by Kathy Merlock Jackson. Jackson: University Press of Mississippi, 2006, pp. 89–90.
10. Quoted in Barrier. *The Animated Man*, p. 26.
11. Quoted in Greene. *Inside the Dream*, p. 21.
12. Quoted in Greene. *Inside the Dream*, p. 23.
13. Thomas and Johnston. *The Illusion of Life*, p. 37.
14. Quoted in Thomas. *Walt Disney*, p. 84.
15. Quoted in Thomas. *Walt Disney*, p. 87.
16. Quoted in Bob Thomas. *Disney's Art of Animation: From Mickey Mouse to Beauty and the Beast*. New York: Hyperion, 1991, p. 12.
17. Quoted in "Walt Disney Quotes." Just Disney.
18. Quoted in Thomas. *Walt Disney*, p. 92.
19. Quoted in Greene. *Inside the Dream*, p. 40.
20. Quoted in Frank Rasky. "80 Million a Year from Fantasy." *Star Weekly* (Toronto), November 14, 1964, p. 9.

Chapter 2: A New Art Form

21. Quoted in Thomas and Johnston. *The Illusion of Life*, p. 41.

22. Quoted in Barrier. *The Animated Man*, p. 92.
23. Quoted in Jackson. *Walt Disney.* "How the Silly Symphonies and Mickey Mouse Hit the Up Grade," p. 3.
24. Quoted in Barrier. *The Animated Man*, p. 86.
25. Quoted in Anel Muller. "Exhibition Exchange: The Silly Symphonies." The Walt Disney Family Museum, September 15, 2011. www.waltdisney .org/content/exhibition-exchange -silly-symphonies.
26. Thomas and Johnston. *The Illusion of Life*, p. 86.
27. Quoted in Thomas. *Disney's Art of Animation*, p. 47.
28. Quoted in Thomas. *Disney's Art of Animation*, p. 60.
29. Quoted in Greene. *Inside the Dream*, p. 60.
30. Quoted in Thomas and Johnston. *The Illusion of Life*, p. 39.

Chapter 3: A Caricature of Life
31. Quoted in Jim Korkis. "What Walt Said." Mouse Planet, June 29, 2011. www.mouseplanet.com/9661/What _Walt_Said.
32. Quoted in Wade Sampson. "More Walt's Words." Mouse Planet, October 14, 2009. www.mouseplanet.com October/9010/More_Walts_Words.
33. Quoted in Thomas. *Disney's Art of Animation*, p. 70.
34. "Academy Awards." Disney Dreamer. www.disneydreamer.com/WDAW October.htm.
35. Quoted in Greene. *Inside the Dream*, p. 53.
36. Quoted in Barrier. *The Animated Man*, p. 153.
37. Thomas and Johnston. *The Illusion of Life*, p. 185.
38. Quoted in Greene. *Inside the Dream*, p. 62.
39. Quoted in Greene. *Inside the Dream*, p. 64.
40. Quoted in Greene. *Inside the Dream*, p. 66.
41. Quoted in Thomas. *Walt Disney*, p. 167.

Chapter 4: Many Mediums
42. Quoted in *Walt & El Grupo*. Documentary film written and edited by Theodore Thomas. Walt Disney Productions, 2009.
43. Quoted in *Walt & El Grupo*.
44. Alfred Charles Richards Jr. *Censorship and Hollywood's Hispanic Image: An Interpretive Filmography, 1936–1955*. Westport, Conn.: Greenwood, 1993, p. 274.
45. Quoted in Thomas. *Walt Disney*, p. 179.
46. Quoted in Greene. *Inside the Dream*, p. 85.
47. Quoted in Thomas. *Walt Disney*, p. 204.
48. Quoted in "Background." Songofthe South.net. www.songofthesouth.net /movie/background.html.
49. Quoted in Jim Korkis. "Walt and the True-Life Adventures." The Walt Disney Family Museum, February 9, 2012. www.waltdisney.org/content /walt-and-true-life-adventures.
50. Quoted in Jackson. *Walt Disney.* "Interview with Stan Hellenk," p. 80.
51. Quoted in Greene. *Inside the Dream*, p. 95.

Chapter 5: A Source of Joy

52. Quoted in Jerry Beck. "Disney Interview in TV Guide (1961)." Cartoon Brew, August 11, 2010. www.cartoonbrew.com/disney/disney-interview-in-tv-guide-1961-26537.html.

53. Steve Biodrowski. "Captain Nemo Double Bill." *Cinefantastique*, August 25, 2007. www.cinefantastiqueonline.com/2007/08/hollywood-gothique-captain-nemo-double-bill.

54. Quoted in Thomas. *Walt Disney*, p. 244.

55. Quoted in "Walt Disney Quotes." Just Disney.

56. Quoted in "Walt Disney's Disneyland." Just Disney. www.justdisney.com/walt_disney/biography/w_disneyland.html.

57. Quoted in "Walt Disney Quotes." Just Disney.

58. Quoted in Greene. *Inside the Dream*, pp. 148–149.

59. Quoted in Thomas. *Walt Disney*, p. 328.

60. Quoted in Thomas. *Walt Disney*, p. 355.

Glossary

animation: Filming a sequence of gradually changing drawings, photographs, or computer-generated images, so that they appear to move.

audio-animatronics: Lifelike three-dimensional figures that move and make sounds.

caricature: A drawing that comically exaggerates somebody's or something's prominent features.

cels: Transparent celluloid sheets that are drawn on, layered, and photographed to produce a moving cartoon.

documentary: An educational film.

family entertainment: Entertainment aimed at both adults and children.

film distributor: A company or person responsible for releasing films to theaters.

film frame: One of many images recorded on film that compose a complete movie.

film producer: The person who puts together and coordinates every aspect involved in making a movie.

imagineer: A term coined by Walt Disney to refer to an artist who combines imagination with engineering skills.

in-betweeners: Artists who produce drawings that are placed between movement poses to create the illusion of continuous, smooth action in animation.

live action: Film or video with real people, animals, and things, in contrast to the created images in animated film and video.

metronome: A mechanical device used to indicate tempo.

multi-plane camera: A film camera used in animation that photographs artwork at different speeds and at different distances to produce a three-dimensional look.

psychedelic art: Art characterized by wild images and colors similar to images experienced by someone under the influence of mind-altering drugs.

sound stage: A large soundproof hangar-like structure where movies are filmed.

For More Information

Books

John Canemaker. *Walt Disney's Nine Old Men and the Art of Animation*. New York: Disney Editions, 2001. A look at the lives and artwork of each of Disney's Nine Old Men.

Christopher Finch. *The Art of Walt Disney*. New York: Abrams, 2011. First published in 1973, this large book looks at Disney's artistic innovations with lots of full-color artwork from his films.

Walter Gitlin. *Walt Disney: Entertainment Visionary*. Minneapolis: Abdo, 2009. This biography examines Disney's life, family, childhood, career, and his most famous works.

Don Hahn. *The Alchemy of Animation: Making an Animated Film in the Modern Age*. New York: Disney Editions, 2008. A step-by-step guide to making animated films, with information about the roles of the different artists involved.

Monique Petersen. *The Little Big Book of Disney*. New York: Disney Editions, 2001. This book contains full-color art, profiles on different Disney artists, behind-the-scenes information about the creation of Disney characters and films, Disney trivia, and fun facts.

Websites

Disney (www.disney.com). This website provides film clips, games, interactive artwork, information about Disney characters and theme parks, and a section called Disney Legends (www.disney.go.com/disneyinsider /history/legends/about), containing numerous articles on the artists involved in creating Disney films.

Disney History Institute (www.disney historyinstitute.com) A blog authored by Disney historian Paul F. Anderson, with information about the history of Disney's films and theme parks, old newspaper articles, photographs, and numerous relevant links.

ImaginNations (www.disneyimagi nations.com). The Disney studio sponsors an Imagineering design competition for students, and this website provides details about the competition, entry forms, and video clips and other information about Imagineering.

MichaelBarrier.com (www.michael barrier.com). This is the website of Michael Barrier, author and Disney historian. There are lots of articles about Disney's work, anima-tion, interviews with Disney artists, photo essays, and links.

The Walt Disney Family Museum (www.waltdisney.org). This is the website for a museum all about Disney that is run by Walt's daughter Diane. The blog has many interesting articles about Disney's life and work, with lots of color photos.

Index

Picture Credits

About the Author

Barbara Sheen is the author of more than seventy books for young people. She lives in New Mexico with her family. In her spare time she likes to swim, cook, garden, and walk. She grew up watching *The Mickey Mouse Club* and Walt Disney's animated films. Writing this book made her realize what a genius Walt Disney was and gave her a new appreciation for the art of animation.